Women, Marriage and Wealth

Women, Marriage and Wealth
The Impact of Marital Status on the Economic Well-Being of Women Through the Life Course

by

Joyce A. Joyce, Ph.D.

Gordian Knot Books

An Imprint of Richard Altschuler & Associates, Inc.
New York

Women, Marriage and Wealth: The Impact of Marital Status on the Economic Well-Being of Women Through the Life Course. Copyright© 2007 by Joyce A. Joyce. For information contact Richard Altschuler & Associates, Inc., at 100 West 57th Street, New York, NY 10019, RAltschuler@rcn.com or (212) 397-7233.

Library of Congress Control Number: 2006933369
CIP data for this book are available from the Library of Congress

ISBN-13: 978-1-884092-68-8
ISBN-10: 1-884092-68-3

Gordian Knot Books is an imprint of the publisher Richard Altschuler & Associates, Inc.

All rights reserved. No part of this publication may be reproduced, stored in a retrieval system, or transmitted, in any form or by any means, electronic, mechanical, photocopying, recording, or otherwise, without written permission of Richard Altschuler & Associates, Inc.

Cover Design and Layout: Josh Garfield

Printed in the United States of America

Distributed by University of Nebraska Press

Dedication

This book is dedicated to my husband and best friend, Jerry Joyce.

Acknowledgements

I would like to thank my editor, Richard Altschuler, for the enormous amount of assistance he gave me throughout the process of writing this book. His knowledge and expertise were an integral part of the finished product. I would also like to thank my husband, Jerry, and my children, Adam, Sean, and Andrea, for their unending support and encouragement.

Contents

Preface	ix
Chapter 1: Women, Marriage and Wealth: Introduction and Overview	1
Chapter 2: Research on Women, Marriage and Wealth	29
Chapter 3: Method for Analyzing Data from the Rand Health and Retirement Study	73
Chapter 4: Determinants of the Economic Well-Being Of Women: Findings from the HRS Sample	80
Chapter 5: Discussion and Conclusions	123
References	141
Appendix 1: The Rand Health & Retirement Study	166
Appendix 2: Statistical Tables	173
Index	194

Preface

Throughout the 20th century, the number of Americans 65 years and older grew rapidly, from 3.1 million in 1900 to 35 million in 2000. According to U.S. Census projections, that rate of increase is expected to accelerate, so that by the year 2030, those 65 and older will represent 20 percent of the total U.S. population (U.S. Census, 2005). Since women have a longer life expectancy than men, most of the "elderly" population will be composed of women, and they likely will be unmarried, since women age 65 and older are more likely to be widowed, divorced, or never married than their male counterparts (U.S. Census Bureau, 2005). Furthermore, although women have increased their labor force participation in the past decade, older women are more likely than older men to live in poverty (U.S. Department of Labor, 2007).

It is for this reason—the rapid erosion of economic well-being of women in America, especially elderly women—that I became interested in this phenomenon, and have devoted myself to it for the past several years. As I studied the literature, it became clear that researchers consistently have concluded that an ever-increasing number of women are destined to be in poverty in their later years.

My research also was motivated by interviews I conducted with women over the years, who graciously shared their stories with me. I became acutely aware from these conversations of how vulnerable women are in terms of their financial security, and how such vulnerability is directly related to their marital status, i.e., their experiences varied greatly depending on their marital status, with married women seeming to have the most economic security.

In the following chapters of this book, I mainly focus on this relationship between marital status and the financial security of women through the life course. My analysis shows that the presence or absence of a spouse greatly impacts the sources of income and wealth available to women, and, as a result, generally affects their economic security.

Older women are especially vulnerable, as they are most likely to be widowed or divorced, and thus have fewer sources of income and other assets available to them. Moreover, for women of all marital statuses, I discuss why decisions and circumstances that occur early in life have a direct impact on economic outcomes later in life.

Women are more likely than men, for example, to work in part-time employment, to interrupt their careers during the years they are raising their children, and to care for an aging parent or spouse. Thus, they receive less income from pensions and Social Security retirement benefits in their later years.

For older individuals, economic security is based not only on income, of course, but also on accumulated assets. I therefore examined the impact of marital status on wealth, which I conventionally define in terms of home ownership, savings and checking accounts, and other financial resources available to individuals and couples. Accumulated wealth prevents or delays the descent into poverty, especially when incomes decrease because of an adverse event such as job loss, health problems, or family changes.

While the impact of marital status on the economic security of women is the main focus of this book, I also took into account other factors that may mediate this relationship. These factors include age, ethnicity or race, work history, parental status, and number of children, all of which interact with each other to influence life course outcomes for women.

A major aspect of this book derives from a unique analysis I conducted on the 2002 Rand Advance Data File of the Health and Retirement Study (HRS). Using nationwide data collected from 10,389 women, I examined how martial status impacts the sources of income and wealth available to women age 50 and over who were married, divorced, widowed, or never married.

The findings from the HRS data analysis and prior empirical studies are supplemented in this book by information I collected from women I interviewed during 2007. Their intimate stories help "bring to life" the statistical findings as well as convey the types of situations women of different marital statuses are living through today.

Although the findings presented in this book demonstrate that married women have access to more sources of income and wealth than their unmarried counterparts, and, therefore, have more economic security, current trends threaten the ability of marriage to ensure financial security for women in the near future, especially older women. The collapse of Enron, for example, resulted in thousands of that company's employees and investors losing all of their savings, children's college funds, and pensions. In the corporate world in general, over the last three years there has been a growing list of pension failures, including 20 companies that defaulted on pension funds of more than $100 million each (AARP, 2007).

Several other factors have contributed to the weakened state of the traditional pension system, including the stock market's fall from 2000 through 2002, low interest rates, and a recession that resulted in reduced company earnings. Those individuals most likely to be affected by the upheaval of pensions are presently in their 50s. Although they are not old enough to have earned a large, protected, pension benefit, they do have a few years left to build a "nest egg," before they reach retirement age.

Another major threat to the economic security of older Americans in the near future, especially unmarried women, is the failing Social Security system. Policy makers continue to debate the future of Social Security, with some implying that the institution itself should be radically changed and possibly abolished, given the impending demand on the system from aging "boomers."

The above "gloom and doom" picture is, of course, offset by various positive economic trends, including those for women. Over the past several decades, for example, women increasingly have been working outside the home for income, and in 2006 they constituted 46 percent of the total labor force. The largest percentage of employed women works in management, professional, and related occupations.

In addition, women's incomes have increased relative to men's, though the median weekly earnings of women who work full time is still only 81 percent of men's earnings, with women earning, on average, $600 and men earning, on average, $743

(U.S. Department of Labor, 2007). Furthermore, older women over the age of 55 are remaining in the work force longer. They now compose 15.6 percent of the total female labor force and 46 percent of employed individuals 55 and over (U.S. Department of labor, 2007).

Despite the above trends, however, less than half of the salaried women working in the United States participate in a pension plan. Moreover, a female retiring at age 55 can expect to live another 27.5 years—four more years than a male retiring at the same age.

Savings can increase a woman's chance of having enough money to last during her later years, but women tend to invest more conservatively, and receive lower rates of return from their investments over time, thus reducing the amount of savings they have at retirement (Orman, 2007). Thus, although women have made great strides in attaining financial security in their later years, their futures seem to be more insecure.

Given all of the countervailing tendencies in our society that affect people's economic lives, a clear and comprehensive analysis of the factors that both positively and negatively affect the financial security of women is vitally needed. I hope to have provided that analysis in this book, especially by detailing the impact of marital status on economic well-being, both alone and as modified by women's demographic and background characteristics.

Based on my findings, I also have made policy recommendations that I believe can help to prevent or delay threats to the economic security of all Americans in the near future. In particular, I hope I have contributed to the national dialogue on the looming prospects for older women, especially those who are unmarried, by raising awareness of vital economic and social issues that will impact their financial well-being, and emphasizing the importance of creating new economic policies and institutions to address the impending changes that are certain to adversely affect the lives of tens of millions of "boomers" as they reach "old age" in the early decades of the 21st century.

Chapter 1
Women, Marriage and Wealth: Introduction and Overview

The primary purpose of this book is to describe and analyze the impact of marital status on the economic well-being of women through the life course, from young adulthood to old age, based on both my own and previous research. A second major purpose of the book is to analyze how the relationship between marital status and wealth is mediated for women by various demographic and personal background factors, including age, ethnicity (or "race"), level of education, number of children, and employment history. A third purpose of *Women, Marriage, and Wealth* is to propose recommendations for public policy, based on findings from my research, that can benefit women through the life course, especially in the later years.

As will become clear during the course of the book, the presence or absence of a spouse impacts the sources of income available to women, and thus can profoundly affect their economic security. This is especially true in later life, when most women are either widowed or divorced, and thus have fewer sources of income available to them.

For purposes of discussion in this book, the phrase *economic well-being* refers to financial security measured in terms of both sources of income and net worth. *Net worth* is defined as accumulated assets minus debt. Conceptually, *wealth* refers to accumulated net assets, or the value of one's total possessions and property rights. The more wealth that individuals and families have, the better they are able to maintain their standard of living should income fall because of job loss, health problems, or family changes.

In conducting the research for this book, I focused on and compared women in all four marital status groups: married, divorced, widowed, and single, never-married. In particular, I focused on transitions in marital status, for example, from married to divorced or widowed, since these changes tend to profoundly affect sources of income and thus the economic well-being of women.

While marital status has a profound impact on women's sources of income and economic well-being, this relationship is mediated by a wide variety of "intervening" variables. As mentioned, they include age, ethnicity, employment history, education, and number of children, among other factors. All of them, alone and in combination, help to determine the impact of marital status on the financial security of women through the life course. Thus, to fully understand the issues involved in women's income security, it is necessary to closely examine both manifold differences among women, the changes they experience through the life course (Willson, 2003), and life course patterns.

Women's lives are shaped, to a great extent, by patterns reflected in family, employment, and access to financial sources. The connection between current economic outcomes and previous experience is much more complicated for women than for men. Examining life course patterns among women, therefore, will allow us to better understand the variability in individual experience. Moreover, it will allow us to recognize that later life is shaped by experiences that cumulate through the life course (O'Rand, 1996).

Early life choices and opportunities, for example, such as those involving employment, education, and parenthood, result in consequences that ripple through to later life. These opportunities and choices, in turn, are influenced by social structures and life course events that may have different consequences for women than for men (DeViney, 1995). Current outcomes are influenced both by processes that occur over time, such as parenthood, and events that develop later in life, such as divorce and widowhood (Willson, 2003). The economic status of many poor, older women, therefore, often reflects the cumulative effect of lack of opportunities through the life course for asset accumulation (Choudhury & Leonesio, 1997).

The Impact of Marital Status on Wealth

This section presents a brief overview of important ways that marital status affects sources of income, economic well-being, and wealth among women in America. In keeping with the life course approach, the discussion proceeds in a chronological order of marital status for many, if not most women today, from "single" to married, and then to divorce and widowhood. In this context, it should be mentioned that because of the writer's special concern with the plight of elderly women in society, who experience the most profound economic changes following marital dissolution, I have paid somewhat more attention to the marital status categories of divorce and widowhood in both this section and throughout the book.

Finally, by way of introduction, it should be mentioned that although reference to mediating factors is impossible to avoid when discussing the impact of marital status on economic well-being, I have minimized discussion in this section of variables such as age, ethnicity, education, work history, and parental status, which are the focus of the following section.

Single, Never Married

In general, the economic lives of single, never-married women are the least complex of all marital status groups, in that they have the fewest sources of income, e.g., no Social Security payment or pension related to a spouse. As a result, they often have the least assets, especially in later life, which may possibly derive from savings, income, investments, Social Security, or a job-related pension. These sources of income are supplemented for a relatively small percentage of single, never-married women by a family inheritance.

Over the past several decades, the trend in American society has been towards a later age of first marriage. Thus, more women are single for longer periods of time than ever before in history. Until and if they get married, they are often in school during their young-to-late late twenties, when most young women either rely on their families for income (e.g., an allowance) or on part-time employment income.

In general, women who are single and have never married need to rely solely on their own sources of income. Previous research on never-married women has largely concentrated on single mothers and their economic well-being. Consistently, it has been reported that single mothers occupy the lowest rungs on the socioeconomic ladder (Bauman 2002; Gyamfi, Brooks-Gunn & Jackson 2001), and that single females have suffered the most substantial decline in postretirement income (Rubin & Nieswiadomy 1995). Scant research, however, has compared never-married women with married women or women who are either divorced or widowed.

Marriage

In general, marriage offers women more economic security and wealth compared to other marital statuses, plus many other benefits, such as better health and a positive impact on children (Waite, 1996; Willson & Hardy, 2002). The great majority of women marry at some time in their lives, and often more than once. The first marriage usually occurs while the women are in their twenties. Overall, married women have the most wealth, which is directly proportional to the length of their marriage and the economic status of their husbands. Generally speaking, married women derive income from the most sources, which tend to increase with age, and cumulatively increase the wealth of married women. The married elderly are more likely to receive income from wages, salary, assets, private pensions, and government pensions than the single elderly (Kart, 1997). Evidence suggests that single, elderly women are more likely to receive financial assistance from their adult children (Hurd & Wise, 1989; Pezzin & Steinberg-Schone, 1999).

The economic security of married women is mainly due to their access to income from more sources than unmarried women. In most cases, they have access either to the wage or salary income of their spouses, as well as their own income, if they are in the paid work force. In addition, they have access to the pension and Social Security retirement income of their spouse, as well as their own, as they reach retirement age. A married woman's retirement benefit from Social Security, however, is greater if her benefits are "dually entitled." Dual entitlement means that a woman could receive benefits based on her own lifetime earnings, and as a wife, receive half of her husband's benefits, or as a widow receive one-hundred percent of her husband's benefit (O'Rand & Henretta, 1999).

Marital Dissolution: Divorce and Widowhood

Although both divorce and widowhood signal the end of a marriage, each has various unique consequences for the economic lives of women. The sources of income vary, for example, according to the type of marital disruption, divorce or widowhood, women experience. Also, the mechanisms that result in negative economic consequences are different for women who experience divorce or widowhood.

The various sources of income that women receive after marital dissolution largely determine their subsequent economic well-being. An examination of access to Social Security, private pensions, amount of savings, and assets reveals the inequality women experience. Financial assistance from adult children, however, can possibly offset financial differences and result in a more equal distribution of wealth for women who have lost a spouse.

Knowing the proportion that each of these income sources contributes to the economic lives of women, therefore, will help to accurately determine the risk of poverty after a marital dissolution. Greater knowledge of them also would further our understanding of the mechanisms in place that determine financial outcomes for women through the life course.

Although the economic experiences of divorced and widowed women differ in many respects, studies on both types of marital dissolution suggest that women face an increased risk of being poor or falling into poverty, regardless of the type of marital dissolution they experience (Choi, 1992; Holden, Burkhauser, & Myers, 1986; Holden & Kuo, 1996; Holden & Smock, 1991; Morgan, 1981, 1989; Smith & Zick, 1986; Smock, et. al., 1999; Stroup & Pollock, 1999). The average age range of divorced and widowed women differs, however, which has implications for economic well-being, such as ongoing employment opportunities and income earning. Older women are more likely to become widowed and younger women are more likely to divorce, because the latter usually occurs in the early to middle stages of married life, when most women are young or middle aged, while widowhood most frequently occurs during both the later years and stages of married life (Morgan, 1989).

While empirical studies have established that a change in marital status from married to either divorced or widowed has both immediate and prolonged negative consequences for the economic well-being of women, it is also true that different researchers have used both diverse measures of economic status and varied definitions of "economic well-being." The most commonly used measures of income and poverty status reflect economic resources at a given point in time, but they have been defined differently across studies, and thus do not adequately reflect differences in sources of financial support in place among older women (Hao, 1996; Street & Wilmot, 2001; Wilmoth & Koso, 2002). Furthermore, the processes by which changes in economic status occur after a marital dissolution are quite different for women who experience either divorce or widowhood (Wilmoth & Koso, 2002).

In terms of consumption and savings, evidence suggests that prior to divorce, consumption increases while savings decreases, in anticipation of the division of household wealth (Fethke, 1984). Both the legal costs of divorce and the process of dividing assets, however, may leave divorced individuals with little household equity and savings (Fethke, 1989). In contrast to this explanation, the life-cycle model of savings predicts that couples increase savings in anticipation of future events (Flavin, 1981)—although the death of a spouse may be an unexpected event—and that individuals should be better prepared financially for the death of a spouse (Wilmoth & Koso, 2002).

Becoming a widow necessarily involves short-term costs, potential loss of income, lost wages, and reduced benefits, but it is also true that housing equity and other assets usually are the property of the surviving spouse (Wilmoth & Koso, 2002). In addition, Social Security survivor benefits may financially protect the surviving spouse (Morgan, 1991). Thus, overall the impact of divorce may be more detrimental than the impact of widowhood on the economic well-being of women.

Divorce

The economic picture for divorced women is often somewhat more complicated than it is for single, never-married and even married women. They may have their own wage and salary income, if they are still in the paid work force, and their own Social Security retirement and pension income, when they reach retirement age. Pension income from an ex-spouse may or may not be available to a woman who is divorced. Federal law, however, has provided for splitting of accrued pension rights in the case of divorce (Goodfellow & Scheiber 1993), and spouses are eligible for the spousal benefit at retirement age, if the couple remained married for ten years (O'Rand & Henretta, 1999).

Previous studies of the impact of divorce on women have been concentrated in several distinct areas, and studies focusing on younger people have been and continue to be quite prevalent. Some researchers have focused on the consequences of divorce for the children in the family (Garfinkle & McLanahan, 1986; Garfinkle, et. al. 1989; Lillard & Waite, 1993), along with the general consequences of the increase of single-mother households (Bianchi, 1995; Burkhauser, et. al., 1991; Cherlin, 1992).

The majority of the research on divorce, however, emphasizes the economic consequences of divorce for women. Holden and Smock (1991), in their extensive review of the literature, found that longitudinal studies of divorce (as well as of widowhood) resulted in negative and prolonged consequences for women's economic well-being. Furthermore, for some subgroups of women, these negative consequences were even more detrimental. Duncan and Hoffman (1985), for example, found that approximately four percent of white women with above-median family incomes while married became poor after divorce but one-third of black women and one-fifth of white women with below-median family incomes during marriage fell into poverty in the year following martial disruption.

Duration of time after divorce also has been shown to have major implications for women. Most studies indicate that negative consequences for the economic well-being of women are prolonged at least five years after marital disruption (Duncan & Hoffman, 1985; Peterson, 1989; Stirling, 1989). Stirling (1989), however, reported no improvement during the first five years following disruption, and Duncan and Hoffman (1985) reported a relatively moderate increase of improvement during the first five years after divorce.

Despite researchers' attention to divorced women, few studies have focused on divorce among the elderly. Although few elderly couples divorce compared with younger couples, the number is still impressive. It has been estimated that each year at least 50,000 persons older than sixty years of age divorce—and their marriages had been thirty to forty years long (Cain, 1988). Evidence suggests these numbers will increase in the future (Uhlenberg & Myers, 1981). In recent years, it has been estimated that about one-fifth of all divorces have involved women over the age of forty, with most of the divorces obtained by women between the ages of forty and sixty (Uhlenberg & Myers. 1981).

The economic consequences of divorce for the elderly, however, cannot be underestimated. In their study of white, elderly divorced individuals, Stroup and Pollock (1999) found that divorced elderly women have significantly lower family incomes than their married counterparts—about twenty-eight percent less. The findings especially support the greater economic disadvantage among women in the lower socio-economic status (SES) levels (Stroup & Pollock, p. 63). This study, however, compared the losses of both men and women. Since negative economic consequences have been shown to be consistently greater for women (Holden & Smock, 1991; Morgan, 1990; Smock, et. al., 1999; Stroup & Pollock, 1999), a comparison of the characteristics of women who have experienced divorce in later life would be a better predictor of the impact of divorce on women.

Widowhood
Previous studies overwhelmingly suggest that older widows constitute a large proportion of women in poverty in old age (Holden, Burkhauser, & Feaster, 1988; Holden, Burkhaser, & Myers, 1986; Hungerford, 2001; Hurd & Wise, 1989; O'Bryant & Morgan, 1989; Vartanian and McNamara, 2002). Several different factors, however, impact the economic outcomes of women who have experienced the death of a spouse. In other words, there are differences in how these women have come to be at such risk of poverty.

In particular, the *time* of this major transition has the most impact. Burkhauser et al. (1991) found that most widows experience a dramatic drop in economic well-being, and are more likely to fall into poverty, during the period that immediately follows the death of their husbands. This phenomenon is further affected by age, for when a wife is over the age of sixty at her husband's death, her risk of poverty is significantly lower (Holden, et. al., 1988). This finding suggests that age eligibility for receipt of Social Security benefits may have an important effect on poverty among recent widows.

Social Security survivor benefits, however, do not effectively prevent poverty among elderly widows, according to several studies. Bound, Duncan, Laren, and Oleinick (1991) concluded, in their analysis of data from the Panel Study of Income Dynamics (PSID), that the economic status of women prior to widowhood is "the strongest predictor of status during widowhood" (p. 115); Holden, Burhauser, and Myers (1986) reported that poor widows were more likely to have been poor before their husband's death, based on data from the Retirement History Study (RHS); and Hurd and Wise (1989) found a strong relationship between prior income of the married couple and the poverty status of the widow. Considering the change in wealth when the husband dies, Hurd and Wise found that enough family wealth was lost to result in the widows becoming poor.

The decline in economic wealth among widows is often due to the substantial decrease in private pension income at the husband's death, as well as to the death itself consuming a large fraction of the family wealth. Hurd and Wise (1989), for example, found that while eighty-five percent of the widows in their study were poor if the couple was poor prior to the death of the husband, thirty-seven percent of the widows were subsequently poor even though the couples were not poor. Furthermore, widows who were not poor collected about twice the life insurance benefits as those who were poor. These results suggest that it is the source of economic resources that may strongly impact the risk of poverty for widows, and that multiple sources of income may protect against either poverty or a major decline in household wealth.

An examination of the characteristics of widowed women provides further insight into why some widows experience a fall into poverty after the death of a spouse while others do not. Using data from the PSID, Smith and Zick (1986) examined the influence of six life course variables thought to mediate the negative economic consequences of widowhood, including age at widowhood, years of marriage, and prior work experience. Their results indicate that each of these factors influence the outcomes in markedly different ways. Those who were widowed at younger ages (i.e., fifty years or younger) and older ages (i.e., sixty-two years or over) were found to be less likely to fall into poverty than those widowed between fifty and sixty-two years of age. The researchers' findings suggest younger widows may suffer less severe economic consequences because they are more likely to be employed. For older widows, the results indicate that survivors of longer marriages are less likely to fall into poverty, because the accumulation of wealth during marriage may attenuate the risk of poverty after the death of a spouse (Smith & Zick, 1986).

Morgan (1981) reports similar findings. In her study of relatively young widows, i.e., under fifty years old, she found that the loss of a spouse did not result in a significant average decline in economic well-being. Her findings suggest, however, that although the amount of income may not have changed dramatically, the source of income did. The widows grew more reliant on Social Security benefits and were working to contribute their own earnings to the household income.

Widowed women in the paid work force rely on their own wage and salary income, and receive Social Security widow benefits, plus possibly some pension income from their deceased husband's pension. However, this is not always the case. Pension and annuity incomes often do not transfer to the spouse after a husband dies; and for women of advanced ages, the pension may be gone, possibly having been taken in a lump sum when they were younger.

Older widows, however, still account for a large proportion of individuals living in poverty. For most people, especially elderly women, Social Security alone is insufficient to guarantee adequate income in later years (Street & Wilmoth, 2001). Moreover, Social Security survivor benefits, which are derived from family status, provide lower income, on average, than benefits based on paid work (Harrington-Meyer, et al., 1994). Adequate income in later years depends on access to private income in the form of a pension, which is least likely to be available to single, older women and minorities, and thus puts them at the greatest relative disadvantage (Street & Wilmoth, 2001).

Psychosocial Effects of Marital Dissolution

Although the focus of this book is on the economic consequences of marital status for women, a few words should be given about the psychosocial effects of marital dissolution on women, because of its importance. Barbara Cain (1988), in her exploratory study of divorce among elderly women, examined how the experiences of these women differ from those of younger women. She found that their unique preexisting attitudes toward marriage complicated adjustment to divorce. They experienced a profound sense of loss, a decrease in self-esteem, and viewed their divorces as similar to the experiences of woman who suffer the sudden death of their spouse after a lengthy marriage. Cain (1988) suggests that these reactions are unique to elderly women who have divorced.

Additional research on the psychosocial dimensions of divorce among the elderly supports these findings. Although divorce is disruptive at any age, older people are most likely to perceive it as a personal failure, because they often operate on an assumption of permanency of marriage. As a result, their expectation of divorce is relatively low (Stroup & Pollock, 1999).

Remarriage

There is agreement among most scholars that remarriage is the most likely route to economic recovery, as income for women who remarry is estimated at twenty-seven percent higher than for those who do not remarry (Duncan & Hoffman, 1985). Remarriage rates in America, however, have been declining and are expected to continue to decline (Glick & Lin, 1986; Uhlenberg, et. al., 1990). Remarriage, therefore, cannot be viewed as a general means to economic recovery for women through the life course.

Factors that Mediate the Impact of Marital Status on The Economic Well-Being of Women

In addition to the effect of marital status on the economic well-being of women, I studied several factors I felt should mediate this relationship, based on previous research. These factors include age, ethnicity (or "race"), work history, education, and parental status, especially number of children. Although each of these factors is discussed under a separate heading, below, it is important to keep in mind that they almost invariably interact among themselves, e.g., a woman's work history and number of children, to form a complex web that affects the relationship between women's marital status and economic well-being through the life course.

Age

Age largely determines sources of income, either from wages and salary during years in the work force or from Social Security and pension as retirement is reached. Generally speaking, younger women have fewer sources of income and less wealth than middle age and older women, especially if they are single. The relationship between age and wealth, however, often reverses as women reach old age, mainly because of marital dissolution. The fact that women live approximately seven more years than men is a mixed blessing, since the risk of falling into poverty increases with age. With non-married women at greater risk of poverty overall, the consequences of divorce or widowhood for older women are more detrimental than for younger women. By the time women reach 65 years of age, their economic lives in general grow more precarious, regardless of their marital status.

In the United States, the elderly have experienced significant improvement in their economic status since the middle of the 20th century because of the Social Security retirement program and the Supplemental Security Income (SSI) program. Nonetheless, the poverty rate remains high among certain segments of the elderly, i.e., those 65 years or older, especially women, blacks, and the oldest old (Choudhury & Leonesio, 1997; Harrington-Meyer, 1990; O'Rand, 1996). Older women, for example, are almost twice as likely to live in poverty as older men (Choudhury & Leonesio, 1997), and their economic vulnerability is directly linked to their greater likelihood of being unmarried (Burkhauser & Duncan, 1989; Harrington-Meyer, 1990; O'Grady-LeShane, 1990).

Marriage, in other words, generally protects elderly women from poverty. Household income data (U.S. Bureau of the Census, 2004) indicate that whereas only five percent of older married women are poor, eighteen percent of older widowed women and twenty-two percent of older divorced women are impoverished. When married women either divorce or become widowed, therefore, they generally experience a decline in their economic well-being, and experience greater economic disadvantage than their married counterparts.

Since Social Security is the main source of income for older women, who are less likely to receive income from private pensions or earnings than are younger women (Street & Wilmoth, 2001), the policy implications are important for the economic well-being of a large segment of the female population.

Ethnicity

The relationship between a woman's marital status and economic security is also affected by her ethnicity, either positively or negatively. Black women, for example, are increasingly likely to never marry, more likely to divorce, and less likely to remarry than are white women (Cherlin, 1992). Black women also spend less of their lives married and are less likely to live with a spouse in old age than white women (Cherlin, 1992, 1998). These racial differences in martial patterns negatively affect income security of black women through the life course (Willson, 2003).

In the past few decades, young black women have postponed marrying or eschewed marrying altogether, but they have not postponed having children, which has contributed to the majority of black households being headed by unmarried women (Cherlin, 1998). While economic inequalities between blacks and whites have prevailed for decades, the increase in single mother black families has substantially raised the level of economic vulnerability of black women. For those who do marry and then experience a marital dissolution, the risks of poverty are higher, since women at risk economically in their marriages face higher rates of poverty after divorce, separation, and widowhood (Morgan, 1991).

In addition, because black women earn less, on average, than their white counterparts, they also are at a much higher risk of experiencing poverty in old age than white women. Although black women are more likely than women of other racial and ethnic groups to be in the paid work force, and although they traditionally work later in their life course, they have substantially lower household income and substantially less growth in income over time (Willson, 2003). Black women are also more likely to work at jobs that pay less, and work part-time compared to white, unmarried women, which results in substantially fewer sources of income for black women in later life.

In contrast to black women who have lost a spouse, white widows are generally older and less willing to seek employment after their marriages end (Morgan, 1989). Black widows, because they are poorer than their white counterparts, and less likely to have access to widow and survivor benefits, more often find it necessary to return to the work force, even though they are close to or past the age of retirement (Williamson & McNamara, 2003). Their unstable work histories and lack of financial resources make it necessary for them to return to the work force past the typical age of retirement. Thus a change in marital status can exacerbate existing inequalities between ethnic groups of women who are widowed.

Employment and Work History

For most women, marriage offers relative financial benefits, but their own employment history also plays an important role in determining their economic security, especially in later life (Willson & Hardy, 2002). Having a spouse, however, directly influences the workforce behavior of married women and, therefore, has a direct effect on their own wages over time.

For most married women, involvement in family life takes precedence over labor force participation, which often results in interrupted work histories. Participation in the paid labor force is especially related to having children, i.e., women with children have the lowest rates of labor force participation (Street & Wilmoth, 2001) and lower lifetime wages. Both the lower rate of employment and lifetime wages mean many women will receive a lower income in older age from governmental programs, pensions, savings, interest, and other sources of income.

For older women, researchers have shown that weak employment histories and marital instability are related to negative economic outcomes. O'Rand and Henretta (1982) found that both married and unmarried women with interrupted employment histories were expected to receive significantly less retirement income than women with more continuous work histories. This variable, i.e., work history, significantly explains the substantial decline in economic well-being most women experience following divorce and widowhood—a decline that is, furthermore, generally prolonged (Duncan & Hoffman, 1985; Holden & Smock, 1991; Morgan, 1991).

For widows, the risk of poverty is directly related to their years of labor market experience. Those with substantial work histories are both less likely to fall into poverty and experience a drastic deterioration of their economic situation (Choi, 1992; Morgan, 1981; Smith & Zick, 1986). The benefits of labor market experience are twofold, for both older and younger widows, especially those who have spent many years working. They may have accumulated financial assets as wage earners that allow them to better deal with the loss of the income of a spouse, and older widows may be eligible for their own Social Security and other retired-worker benefits, which would make them less likely to be poor than those who receive only Social Security survivor benefits and life insurance (Choi, 1992).

For many elderly women, Social Security is the primary or only source of income. Because Social Security benefits are based on working wages, and women's mean monthly earnings are significantly lower than men's (Harrington-Meyer, 1990), a lifetime of weak attachment to the labor force leaves many older women without a spouse ill-prepared for economic security.

Education

For women, work history is generally related to education in a positive way, i.e., women with more years of education tend to have more continuous work histories and to work for a longer duration. These factors result in greater wage and salary income over time, both before and after marriage ends (Choi, 1992; Morgan, 1991; Smock et al., 1999).

Morgan (1991) found a direct correlation between income and education level before and after marital dissolution. Women with higher educational attainment were at lower risk of poverty over time. Results were similar in other research as well (Choi, 1992; Maudlin, 1990; Smock, et. al., 1999; Stroup & Pollock, 1999). In her study of women who remain above the poverty level after divorce, for example, Maudlin (1990) reported that per capita income for the women increased as education increased, regardless of their economic standing following marital disruption. Taking socio-demographic variables into account, the results of studies on elderly women who experienced either divorce or widowhood confirmed the favorable impact of educational attainment on economic outcomes for these women. Stroup and Pollock (1999) found that divorced women with professional or technical backgrounds have significantly higher family incomes than women in less prestigious labor categories.

This relationship between education and income, however, is less apt to hold for women who have experienced marital disruption, according to Choi (1992), who found that elderly divorced women with substantial work histories were still more likely to be poor compared to widows with less substantial work histories.

In general, because higher educational attainment is directly related to higher income, women with higher educational attainment are at a lower risk of poverty over time (Morgan, 1991). Furthermore, per capita income for women has been shown to increase as education increases (Maudlin, 1990). Conversely, women with a lower rate of employment and lower wages are certain to receive less income in older age, since Social Security is based on working wages. Education is also important as a buffer against the negative economic consequences of a marital disruption, by better enabling women to find employment.

Number of Children

Another mediating factor to consider, in examining the impact of martial status on the economic well-being of women, is that of having children. In general, having children can both directly and indirectly impact women's earnings (Hatch, 1990). Studies consistently indicate that women's childrearing responsibilities are related to negative economic consequences in later life, though not necessarily during earlier stages of the life course.

O'Rand & Landerman (1984) reported that for each child a woman has, and for each year she delays entering into full-time labor force participation, her occupational status is reduced and, subsequently, her income in later life. Moreover, the number of children a woman has is inversely related to her lifetime earnings, i.e., the greater the number of children, the lower the lifetime earnings (Hatch, 1990).

As discussed above, prior labor-market experiences affect the ability of women to deal with economic hardships after either divorce or widowhood. We can, therefore, hypothesize that women who have had children will be more at risk of poverty than women who have not had children following a marital disruption. This relationship needs to be more extensively examined, and would further our understanding of the mechanisms related to women's descent into poverty, especially in later life.

Theoretical Framework

In this book, I use a theoretical framework to help explain, understand, and predict relationships for women that involve marital status, economic well-being, and mediating factors. The framework derives from a synergistic approach based on elements from three perspectives, namely, the Life Course, Feminist, and Political Economy of Aging perspectives. Each of these is now briefly described.

Life Course Perspective

In life course research, two key concepts are "trajectories" and "transitions," which are interrelated. Individual life courses are trajectories characterized by both long-term patterns of stability, change and multiple transitions, and they develop within particular social and economic contexts (George, 1993). Transitions refer to changes in an individual's status, such as divorce or widowhood that are discrete and occur along a trajectory (Elder, 1995).

When employing the life course perspective, one's emphasis is on interactions between individual trajectories and structural contexts, the interdependence of various life events and their resulting pathways, and the links between early and late events through the life course (Elder, 1985; O'Rand, 1996). While studying individuals, researchers can discern the effects of transitions at one point in time on subsequent life course outcomes. The emphasis of investigation is on processes by which early transitions may influence later life patterns (George, 1993).

Using this approach, researchers can understand women's economic well-being in later life in the context of their individual choices through the life course, such as decisions about marriage, education, childbearing, and labor force activity; the structural contexts within which these decisions are made, such as opportunities for education, women's lower wage earnings, and availability of jobs; and the transitions that women experience, such as divorce or widowhood.

Another core premise of the life course paradigm is that the processes and outcomes individuals experience are shaped by the historical times and societal mechanisms within which they occur (Elder, 1995). The life course of individuals, in other words, is shaped in accordance with terms established by a larger society. This premise provides an important link for understanding the experiences of women. The structural contexts within which women make their decisions are central to the discussion throughout the remainder of this book.

Political Economy of Aging Perspective

The political economy of aging theoretical framework is an approach that recently has gained considerable attention, especially in dealing with issues of social policy. It highlights structural influences on aging, and emphasizes the relevance of social struggles embedded in power relations (Estes, Linkins, & Binney, 1996). According to this perspective, political and economic forces account for the distribution of societal resources in ways that maintain or increase inequality on the basis of class, race, or gender. For older individuals, the structure of income sources is grounded in a conceptualization of family status that is permanent. Retirement wage programs are based on a traditional family model, i.e., one with a male breadwinner and a dependent, female, family caregiver. After a lifetime of unpaid or underpaid labor, many older women without a spouse are left ill-prepared for economic security (Street & Wilmoth, 2001).

This framework recognizes the structural influences on aging that intersect with social class, race, and gender, and their direct impact on the resources individuals may draw from in old age (Estes et al., 1996).

The Feminist Perspective

The feminist approach illuminates the gendered nature of society. It emphasizes the different ways men and women experience aging, and how gender-related differences are related to the distribution of resources. It also charges that research on women is often based on a conceptual model derived from men's experience, and that women are measured against a masculine model.

The feminist approach is especially effective for analyzing societal structures and practices that produce both gender differentiation and inequalities. In the United States, deeply entrenched ideologies about age and gender have enormous consequences for opportunity structures available to men and women at different stages of the life course. The socially constructed nature of gender affects the life chances of individuals, including access to financial resources in old age (Moen, 1996). Historically, men and women have experienced different attachments to the work force and institutional barriers to social mobility, prestige, power, and income from paid employment. These factors and others result in different experiences for men and women, especially during later stages of the life course (Roos, 1983).

According to the feminist perspective, the role of the state also profoundly affects older women's income security, helps to sustain the subordination of women, and exemplifies an important aspect of the political economy of aging (Estes et al., 1996). The governmental programs in place are based on a patriarchal family form—the nuclear family with a male breadwinner and a dependent wife. Women's dependence is reinforced through a spousal wage relationship. Therefore, one of the major causes of poverty for older individuals is inequality that is associated with gender.

Organization of the Remainder of the Book

The remainder of this book is organized into five chapters. In Chapter 2, I provide an in-depth look at the wealth of research studies on how marital status impacts the economic well-being of women at all stages of the life course, both in the United States and cross-culturally, and how this relationship is mediated by demographic and personal background factors. This chapter also provides the context for fully appreciating the findings I present from my unique research on women during the later stages of the life course.

In Chapter 3, I briefly describe the research method I used to conduct my unique empirical analysis of over 10,000 American women, the nature of the data I analyzed, and the hypotheses I formulated and tested, based on the three theoretical perspectives discussed above. In Chapter 4, I present the findings from this analysis, and conclusions for the hypotheses tested. I conclude the book in Chapter 5 with a discussion of the implications of the findings for women through the life course, especially as they pertain to social policy in the United States that directly affects the concerns and needs of elderly women.

Chapter 2
Research on Women, Marriage and Wealth

Researchers in both the United States and other countries have systematically studied women's socioeconomic status in society for more than a century. They have also studied how a wide variety of demographic and social variables, including marital status, have impacted the economic well-being of women. My analysis of a large data set on contemporary women, discussed in the next several chapters, makes a unique contribution to this body of empirical studies that can best be appreciated within the context of prior research on this topic. Thus the purpose of this chapter is both to convey the rich body of information others have revealed through their studies and to provide background and context to fully understand the findings from my empirical research.

In particular, in this chapter I focus mainly on studies that have examined the relationship between women's marital status and wealth, but I also devote some attention to studies that relate various demographic and social variables other than marital status to women's income and wealth. The studies I discuss and synthesize are those I consider both most important and representative of the universe of studies on the subject. Although the focus is on studies of American women, I also discuss research on women outside the U.S., including in Canada, Great Britain, Europe, Africa and Asia, for two major reasons: first, they highlight similarities and differences with findings from U.S. research, and second, they expand our universe of knowledge about relationships between economic variables and marital status, especially in developing and "second world" countries around the globe.

Organizationally, I first discuss comparative studies, i.e., research that compares and contrasts both married and unmarried women—including divorced, widowed, and single, never married women. Next I discuss studies that focus only on women of each marital status, respectively, including studies of married, divorced, widowed, and single, never married women. The third section focuses on research that reveals how demographic and social variables affect women's income, wealth, and financial security irrespective of their marital status, with the emphasis on later stages of the life course. At the end of the chapter, I summarize and synthesis the findings from the studies and discuss their implications for both my own statistical analysis and the future of women's economic well-being at the beginning of the 21st century.

Comparative Studies of Married and Unmarried Women

Research studies that compare married and unmarried women—including divorced, widowed, and never married women—shows most clearly the economic advantages marriage affords women compared to any other marital status. These studies also point out a variety of behavioral, attitudinal, and other differences between the marital status groups. In this section, I discuss several of the most important comparative studies, beginning with research on women in the United States.

A variety of researchers have conducted studies to determine the relationship between marital status, income, and wealth. Hirschl, Altobelli, and Rank (2003) sought to estimate the life course incidence and age pattern of affluence among American couples in comparison to nonmarried, never married, and formerly married men and women. They computed life course probabilities from a series of life tables that were built upon 25 years of data from the Panel Study of Income Dynamics (n = 8,510 25-year-olds; n = 3,481 45-year-olds). The results confirmed the notion that marriage enhances the lifetime probability of affluence, and that this advantage varies sharply by both gender and race. According to the researchers, the findings suggest that the marital advantage for gaining affluence is textured by a financial landscape of gender and race inequality.

Wilmoth and Koso (2002) used data from the 1992 Health and Retirement Survey to predict wealth for both women and men, using separate ordinary least squares (OLS) regression models for each sex. The results indicated that individuals who were not continuously married had significantly lower wealth than those who remained married throughout the life course. In addition, the findings showed that remarriage offsets the negative effect of a marital dissolution. From the findings, the researchers concluded that accounting for the sequence of marital events provides a detailed picture of the life paths that lead to wealth heterogeneity, especially among the older population.

Pollock and Stroup (1996) conducted a study to test Lenore Weitzman's (1985) claim that women, as well as men, lose economic well-being in the first year after divorce. To conduct the test, the researchers compared family income data for married and divorced women and men taken from General Social Surveys, 1972-1991, across five socioeconomic status categories. The findings, based on t-tests, revealed that incomes of divorced women were lower than those of married women. The same finding also applied to men.

Goetting et al. (1995) used data from the Georgia Centenarian Study to investigate sources and amounts of financial resources among women aged 60-90, and their perception about the adequacy of those resources. The findings indicated that marital status, as well as age and race, had an impact on women's financial resources. Most important, the researchers found that over twice as many married women received pensions, and that more of them had investment earnings, than women who were not married. Fourteen times as many single women as married women were in poverty. In addition, the researchers found that centenarian women had the highest poverty rate. Six times as many black as white women received Supplemental Security Income, and the poverty rate for black women approached that of single centenarian women.

DeViney and Solomon (1995) used a sample of retired women and men from the Social Security Administration's Master Beneficiary Record to test theoretical explanations for gender differences in retirement income. The researchers believed theories of human capital/status attainment, dual economy, and labor-market segmentation helped to explain differences in retirement income between men and women, but they also felt these factors did not totally eliminate the influence of gender. They found that only the family demand factor, representing the continuity of marital career substantially, reduced the effect of being a woman. The most important finding of their study was that women who were currently and continuously married to the same man received more retirement income than women who had experienced divorce or widowhood.

Schuchardt and Guadagno (1991) examined the income, sources of income, expenditures, and demographic characteristics of lower-middle-income two-parent families and single-mother families, using data from the 1987 Consumer Expenditure Survey. The researchers underscored the reality of financial instability faced by many two-parent families at lower income levels. In this study, the subjects were renters and not fully attached to the labor force. The findings showed that two-parent families received proportionately more income from wage and salary earnings, and that single mothers were more dependent on public assistance and alimony or child support. For both family types, nearly 75% of family expenditures were for housing, food, and transportation.

Cross Cultural Comparative Studies of Married and Unmarried Women

As mentioned above, studies on women in foreign countries can enable us to more fully understand the impact of marital status on American women's economic well-being and other aspects of life, as well as similarities and differences in these relationships across cultures.

Several studies have compared married and unmarried women in a cross-cultural context as regards the relationship between their income status and health status. In one study of single and married mothers in Canada and Norway, Curtis and Phipps (2004) found that the health status of single mothers was worse than that of married mothers in Canada but not in Norway. Even controlling for demographic characteristics and health behaviors in Canada, the researchers found that the health status of single mothers was worse. However, only after controlling for income did the differential in health status between married and single mothers in Canada disappear. An important difference between the countries, according to the researchers, is that single mothers in Norway were much less likely to be poor compared to their counterparts in Canada, because they received more generous social transfers.

In another study, Janzen and Muhajarine (2003) noted that social role researchers have increasingly gone beyond simply asking whether role occupancy is associated with health status, and were focusing on clarifying the context in which particular social role-health relationships emerge. Building on this perspective, Janzen and Muhajarine investigated the relationship between social role occupancy and health status over time in a sample of employed Canadian women and men who varied by family role occupancy, life stage, and income adequacy. According to the researchers, the findings indicated that compared to "triple-role women"—defined as those who are married, have children living at home, and are in the workforce—single and double-role occupants in 1994/95 were significantly more likely to report poorer self-rated health and the presence of a chronic health condition in 1996/97. The researchers, further, found that this relationship held true for women in varying life stage and economic circumstances, and that family role occupancies were not as strongly related to the health status of men as of women.

Byles, Feldman, and Mishra (1999) contrasted the health and social needs of 12,624 married and widowed older women, aged 70-75, who completed baseline questionnaires for the Australian Longitudinal Study on Women's Health. Among the research participants, 34.5% were widowed, with 13.5% widowed within the previous 12 months. The findings showed that recently widowed women had particular physical and mental health needs as well as financial and practical needs related to income management. They had the lowest self-rated health, were most likely to report they were stressed about their health, and scored significantly lower than married women on all eight subscales of the SF-36. Anther important finding was that widows, compared to married women, were more likely to experience stress from relationships with children or other family members.

Davies and Denton (2002) compared the economic well-being of women who were married and women who divorced or separated in mid or later life, using 1994 data from Statistics Canada's Survey of Labor and Income Dynamics. The researchers measured economic well-being by adjusted economic family total money income, before-tax low-income cut-offs, and ownership of dwelling. The research participants included two groups who were compared: (a) women and men aged 65 and over still in their first marriages, and (b) women and men aged 65 and over who were divorced or separated at age 45 or older. The results showed that women who became divorced or separated in mid or later life were more likely to have low income than either married persons or men who became divorced or separated in mid or later life. In addition, persons who divorced or separated in mid or later life were less likely than married persons to live in a dwelling owned by a member of the household. Regression analyses also showed that receiving pension income and receiving earnings were positively associated with income for women who became divorced or separated in mid or later life.

Studies of Married, Divorced, Widowed, and Never Married Women

In this section I discuss studies that focus solely on women of each respective marital status, starting with married women and following with studies on divorced, widowed, and single, never married women.

Married Women

More than a decade ago, Waite (1996) noted that, despite a decline in the popularity of marriage, evidence demonstrates that many benefits accrue from being married, including: (a) greater wealth and higher wages; (b) better health and increased longevity; (c) improved intimacy and sexuality; and (d) the beneficial impact of marriage on children, including greater likelihood of completion of high school education and lowered likelihood of living in poverty. Marriage appears to produce these benefits through four mechanisms: (a) partners joining in a long-term contract; (b) the creation of coinsurance stemming from shared economic and social resources; (c) economies of scale; and (d) connection of individuals to other individuals, groups, and social institutions that provide benefits and give life meaning.

One study showed that a woman's income is also a basis for her degree of power within the marital relationship. Biddlecom and Kramarow (1998) noted that being "head of the household" historically has been equated with being the main economic provider, a status traditionally occupied by men. In their study, however, the researchers used a change in the U.S. Census definition of household headship to examine whether headship for married women was associated with being the primary breadwinner versus other noneconomic explanations, using microdata from the 1990 U.S. Census. Their findings indicated that women who were the main income providers in a marriage were much more likely to be household heads than were women in coprovider marriages. There was also support from the data for an egalitarian ideology explanation: when both spouses are highly educated, the wife is more likely than the husband to be household head, net of her relative economic independence in that marriage. Yet, the force of convention remains strong, given the low prevalence of headship among married women. The researchers also noted that they used the new census definition partly to reflect the changing economic status of women, but the reality is that conventional gender behaviors persist in household headship.

Teachman, Tedrow and Crowder (2000) agreed that being married generally offers women advantages economically over other marital statuses, but they also argued that marriage has been declining over the past several decades as a basis of women's economic stability. To them, the declining prevalence of early marriage, increasing level of marital dissolution, and growing tendency of women to never marry, especially among minority groups, reflect changes in the relative economic prospects of women (as well as men), and support the conclusion that marriage is becoming less valued as a source of economic solidity. Paralleling these trends have been sharp changes in the economic stability of families, characterized most notably by a growing importance of women's income and increasing economic inequality among American families.

In this vein, Hogan, Perrucci, and Behringer (2005) found that marriage is not always beneficial for all women. In their research—based on ordinary least squares (OLS) regression models, which predicted logged employment income for whites still working in late career—they found that marriage yielded no significant earnings advantages for the women. (The researchers also found the same result for the variables union membership and managerial and professional occupations.) Data for this study came from women surveyed in the first wave (1992) of the Health and Retirement Study. In contrast to the women, the researchers found that white men reaped earnings benefits on all the variables. For the men, however, these variables were additional to benefits of self-employment combined with either marriage or professional occupation. Based on the findings, the researchers suggested that the enduring inequality between women and men is rooted in relations between the sexes—especially marriage and the types of relationships between men, such as closed-status communities or "old boy" networks.

Other research has focused on factors that affect married women's decisions to work for income. Edwards (2001), for example, attempted to elaborate on conventional explanations for the rapid employment growth of married mothers of preschoolers, by testing the hypothesis that variation in the pursuit of home ownership had affected this trend for different decades since the 1950s. Methodologically, Edwards compared hypothetical and observed trends since 1970, by measuring husbands' income in terms of mortgage qualification, and using logistic regression analysis of pooled Current Population Survey data to estimate trends standardized for compositional change. The results showed that the declining ability of husbands' income to qualify for mortgages and the rising educational attainment of mothers explained the post-1970 accelerated employment growth for mothers of preschoolers. By the 1980s, other influences had greater relative effects on young mothers' employment. Based on the findings, Edwards concluded that home ownership contributed to slower growth in preschoolers' mothers' employment through the 1950s and 1960s, raising standard-of-living expectations. Declining affordability in the 1970s inspired even more rapid growth. Pursuit of prescribed standards of living has increasingly motivated families to embrace dual-earner work and family arrangements.

According to Shaw's (1992) study on married women's employment, in a life-cycle model of married women's labor supply, husbands' expected lifetime income rather than current income should have a greater effect on wives' labor supply. Using the Panel Study of Income and Dynamics data, the findings showed that the husbands' average lifetime income (over the panel years) had a greater negative income effect than their current income. Shaw noted, however, that this income effect has declined over time, indicating that the labor supply of wives is becoming less sensitive to their husbands' incomes. According to Shaw, such declining elasticity should cause household income inequality to worsen over time, but it has been offset by other factors.

In another study concerned with the impact of women's employment on marital stability, Tzeng and Mare (1995) tested a hypothesis linking trends in the U.S. labor market and the stability of marriages from the mid-1960s to late 1980s, focusing on changes in married women's employment status (housewife to working spouse) and couples' education and socioeconomic levels. Their data came from the National Longitudinal Surveys of Women (n = 5,159), Youth (n = 12,686), and Young Men (n = 5,225), which the researcher subjected to a discrete time hazard model for marriage dissolution. The results showed that a wife's relatively high level of work experience was more likely to create instability than if her level was lower than her husband's, although improvements in the wife's status generally tended to enhance marital instability. Couples with both higher levels of education and stronger attachment to the work force tended to have stable marriages. Husband and wife equality of either educational attainment or income did not affect marriage stability.

Many other researchers also have been concerned with examining marital stability in terms of women's income and income inequality between spouses. In one study, Cancian and Reed (1999) sought to estimate the extent to which rising family income inequality could be explained by changes in married women's earnings. To accomplish this goal, they developed a decomposition equation that both separates single persons from married couples (i.e., decomposition by population group) and, for married couples, distinguishes the impact of wives' earnings from other sources of income (i.e., decomposition by income source). For the analysis, the researchers used income data from the Current Population Survey, 1968-1995. The findings showed that, despite the rising correlation between husbands' and wives' earnings, changes in wives' earnings did not explain a substantial portion of the increase in family income inequality. These results contradicted those of some previous analyses, which the researchers said could be traced to others' use of a variety of conceptually different approaches.

Related to the above, several studies have investigated the relationship between women's income and employment, on the one hand, and marital instability and satisfaction—precursors of divorce—on the other. In a study done a decade ago, Clydesdale (1997) found a relationship between upper income status and marital dissolution among early U.S. "baby boomers" (n = 958). The analysis was based on 1965-1982 interview data from the Youth-Parent Socialization Panel Study for youths who graduated from high school in 1965. The findings revealed, among other things, that possessing an upper income and, especially, rising to upper income status, was associated with a double to quadruple likelihood of divorce.

Rogers and DeBoer (2001) investigated the effects of increases in married women's actual income and in their proportion of total family income on a variety of variables, including the likelihood of divorce, marital happiness, and psychological well-being. The researchers used data from a sample of 1,047 married individuals (not couples) in medium-duration marriages, drawn from a five-wave panel survey begun in 1980 and continuing to 1997. They also used structural equation modeling, to assess the impact of increases in married women's absolute and relative income from 1980 to 1988 on the marital happiness and well-being of married men and women in 1988; and they used event history analysis to determine how these changes affected the risk of divorce between 1988 and 1997. The researchers found that increases in married women's absolute and relative income significantly increased their marital happiness and well-being. Increases in married women's absolute income generally had nonsignificant effects for married men. The researchers found, however, that married men's well-being was significantly lower when married women's proportional contributions to the total family income were increased. The likelihood of divorce was not significantly affected by increases in married women's income. Nevertheless, the researchers concluded that increases in married women's income might indirectly lower the risk of divorce by increasing women's marital happiness.

In another study on income and marital happiness, Rogers (1999) surprisingly found that low marriage quality actually stimulated women to increase their incomes. Rodgers investigated the nature and direction of the relationship between wives' income and marital quality, using panel data for a nationally representative sample of 771 married women and men (not couples) and structural equation modeling. The results of the analysis indicated that increases in wives' income did not significantly affect either husbands' or wives' perceptions of marital discord. Instead, increases in marital discord contributed significantly to increases in wives' income, by increasing the likelihood that nonemployed wives enter the labor force.

In a similar vein, Heckert, Nowak and Snyder (1998) noted that, in the last several decades, a shift had occurred in the relative contributions of married women to household earnings, but wondered about the impact of relative earnings of husbands and wives on the likelihood of marital disruption. To determine this, their study estimated a discrete-time hazard model using data on first-married couples from the 1986-1989 waves of the Panel Study of Income Dynamics. The findings showed that the relative earnings of husbands and wives were a significant predictor of marital disruption, although the relationship was nonlinear. The researchers suggested the nonlinear effect was linked to the varying economic circumstances of different groups of couples.

Researchers also have examined how economic variables within the context of the marital relationship affect many other phenomena central to the lives of married women. Zick, Fan and Chang (2004), for example, conducted a study of medical expenditures for two groups of married women, distinguished by the health status of their husbands, which showed the financial disadvantage of impending widowhood. The researchers noted that, for married couples, prior research had established that the household's needs-adjusted income declines when a spouse dies, but that the process by which this income decline occurs is less clear. They, therefore, decided to study the latter, using the 1996, 1997, and 1998 Medical Expenditure Panel Surveys (MEPS). Specifically, they wanted to learn whether medical expenditures of married women prior to widowhood contributed to the income decline. Using multivariate regression analysis, Zick, Fan and Chang found that both total and out-of-pocket medical expenditures were significantly higher for the about-to-be-widowed women compared to an otherwise similar group of continuously married, healthy women. The differences were particularly large when the soon-to-be-deceased spouse was not eligible for Medicare.

Brandon (1999) sought to determine how economic factors for married mothers—both employed and not employed—have affected their childcare decisions. Specifically, Brandon investigated whether aggregate income alone or a host of other economic variables—such as financial agreements between wives and husbands, cost of childcare, mothers' wages, and sources of income—affected a mother's decision to use childcare. Based on data from the fifth wave of the National Longitudinal Study of the High School Class of 1972 (n = 14,489 respondents in 1986), Brandon found for working mothers that the price of childcare was what mattered, not their wages; for nonemployed mothers, the reverse was true. The researcher, however, found similar patterns for income effects for all mothers. Husbands' incomes did not affect mothers' childcare choices, but mothers' own abilities to pay and sources of nonwage income did. The only detected effect of spousal incomes on wives' childcare choices occurred when husbands pooled their incomes with their wives' incomes. From the study, Brandon concluded that, although market childcare is a collective consumption good, not all wives in two-parent families have access to their husbands' incomes with which to pay for childcare.

Fitzpatrick and Vinick (2003) noted that recent studies have viewed retirement as a family transition that affects others in the close family circle, as well as the retiree, and is a process that occurs over time rather than a single event. The researchers claimed, therefore, that it is important to learn more about how husbands' retirement affects the women with whom male retirees share their lives. According to the researchers, most previous research studied the wives of retirees using cross-sectional designs, and in general, found that husbands' retirement had little effect on wives' marital quality. This study represented an advance over much of the previous research, the researchers claimed, because they used a longitudinal design. Specifically, they examined wives' assessments of marital quality, including contextual life changes before their husbands' retirements, and compared the assessments of the same wives following their husbands' retirements. To study these phenomena, the researchers used data from the Normative Aging Study, including 61 wives prior and subsequent to husbands' retirement. Based on comparison of mean scores and sub-scale scores at both baseline and at Time 2 using the paired t-test, the researchers found positive changes in the "cohesion" sub-scale of wives' scores. This finding suggested to the researchers that shared activities increased after retirement, and that the increase was pleasing to the wives. In addition, multiple regression analysis revealed that changes in both income and husbands' health contributed most to marital quality change among wives, with changes in wives' employment status also contributing. To specify retirement-context conditions including the subscales of satisfaction, cohesion, consensus, and affection, the researchers used additional multiple regression models. The results indicated continuity in wives' marital quality scores both before and after husbands' retirement.

In another study on retirement, Szinovacz and DeViney (2000) assessed the effects of both spouse and marital relationship characteristics on husbands' and wives' retirement decisions and labor force withdrawal. The analyses were based on two waves of the National Survey of Families and Households. The data showed that marital characteristics influenced retirement decisions in several ways. Husbands adjusted their retirement in terms of wives' benefit eligibility, whereas wives' retirement was contingent on the couple's income. Husbands also tended to leave the labor force when their wives were ill. In addition, retirement decisions seemed to reflect considerations about postretirement marital quality and husband's status in the marriage. Gender differences prevailed with regard to the impact of work and marital history on retirement decisions.

Cross Cultural Studies of Married Women

As mentioned above in this section, researchers also have been interested in analyzing relationships between marital status and the economic well-being of women in countries around the world. As can be seen from the few examples provided in this section, the researchers are concerned with examining phenomena similar to those examined for married women in the United States.

Knotter (2004) studied the wives and children of Amsterdam dock laborers, in terms of the husbands' income, plus "poor relief" they received, and plotted these figures against their family cycles, using data from the files of the municipal poor relief institutions. The emerging patterns confirmed results arrived at in American, British, and Belgian studies: Married women worked for wages mainly in the first period of the marriage, when the children were still too young to earn. For the same reason, families relied more on poor relief in this first period than later on. Only in the second and third periods could families rely, more or less, on their own labor, due to the substantial contribution made by their children, from age 14 on. Wives of these casual laborers worked more for wages than did the wives of more skilled laborers. Based on these findings, Knotter concluded that norms and rules about wives' responsibilities in the home obviously were strong enough to prevent women from aspiring to substantial, or even lifetime jobs, although only a few families in the sample could survive on the males' incomes alone.

Bianchi, Casper, and Peltola (1999) used Luxembourg Income Study data to examine married women's dependency on their husbands' earnings in nine Western industrialized countries: Australia, Belgium, Canada, Finland, Germany, the Netherlands, Norway, Sweden, and the U.S. (total n = 37,772). When examining the level and degree of dependency, and the labor force participation of married women across countries, the nine countries fell into the three clusters delineated in Gosta Esping-Andersen's (1990) welfare states typology. When examining determinants of dependency in each country, however, the clustering disappeared. Wives' dependency increased with age, presence of young children, and number of children. It declined, however, when wives' labor force participation and education were high relative to their husbands', and in families that relied more on unearned sources of income. The similarity of patterns across countries suggested that gender differences in the work-family nexus were deeply entrenched in all countries, and continued even in the face of very active social policy to minimize their effects.

In another study of economic dependency, Van Berkel and De Graaf (1998) replicated a study by Sorensen and McLanahan (1987) of U.S. trends in married women's economic dependency, using 1979-1991 Dutch income data for members of 10,090 married couples, in which the wife was age 64 or less. The results showed that, although a vast majority of the Dutch wives were still completely or strongly dependent on their husband's income, their economic dependency was decreasing at a significant rate. Despite clear life course differences that seemed to persist, declining levels of dependency were observed in each age group that primarily seemed to reflect changes in married women's employment status over time.

Del Boca, Locatelli, and Pasqua (2000) used a subsample of 5,868 married couples from the 1995 Bank of Italy Survey to test the relationship between the education and employment status of wives and husbands. Results showed that employed women were likely to be married to employed men with a higher level of education and higher income. The estimates of the labor supply decisions of wives showed that the effect of the unemployment status of husbands was mediated by other factors associated with the family's view of wives working outside the home. According to the researchers, the response to a husband's unemployment depended significantly on the employment decisions of parents (mothers and mothers-in-law), whom the researchers considered to be a proxy for the couple's attitude toward women's work.

Paes de Barros and Pinto de Mendonca (1992) analyzed data from the 1985 Brazilian Annual Household Survey of metropolitan areas to determine whether the labor force participation of married women influenced family-income inequality. The researchers decomposed the marginal impact on family earnings into two components—one generated uniquely by differences in earnings inequality between spouses, and another produced by imperfect assortive mating on spouses' earnings, i.e., mating that indicates a correlation between partners in some character or trait, such as physical beauty, in which the true incidence is greater than chance. The results showed that wives' labor income had a negligible impact on family-income inequality in Brazil, and demonstrated the importance of isolating the influence of imperfect assortive mating from that due to inequality in earnings between men and women.

Divorced Women

Research has shown that formerly married women suffer an income decline after divorce, and that they generally have less wealth than when they were married (Butricia & Iams, 2003; Hanson, McLanahan, & Thomson, 1998; Oygard, 2004; Wang & Amato, 2000. The effect of divorce on income, however, is mediated by demographic, social and psychological characteristics, especially in later life. One study that determined this was conducted by Butrica and Iams (2003). They used projections from the Social Security Administration's Modeling Income in the Near Term (MINT1) to examine the characteristics and retirement income of white non-Hispanic, black non-Hispanic, and Hispanic divorced women in the baby boom cohort. The researchers found significant differences in retirement income for divorced women of different racial and ethnic groups, but the characteristics associated with higher or lower retirement income were very similar: being college educated, owning a home, and having pension and asset income, for example, corresponded to increased retirement income for all racial and ethnic groups. Because black and Hispanic women, however, were less likely than white women to be college educated, to own their home, and to have pension and asset income, their retirement income tends to be lower than that of white women.

Oygard (2004) found that divorced women suffer a decline in income, but also noted that their adjustment to divorce depends on a variety of factors, based on attending divorce support groups, including income, education, level of attachment, counseling with important social network groups, and having or not having a new partner. Oygard's assumption was that personal capital would influence the extent to which participants would benefit from the participation; and that women who were highly educated and least attached to network groups would benefit more from the participation than those who were both less educated and attached. The findings showed that participants who had higher incomes, as well as those who counseled with social network groups to a high extent, benefited more than their counterparts.

Wang and Amato (2000) also found that a decline in income accompanies divorce, but that this variable is not a major cause of difficulty in women adjusting to divorce. Specifically, the researchers analyzed data from 208 individuals who divorced, during a 17-year longitudinal study, to examine factors that predicted adjustment to marital disruption. Using stress and coping theory as a guide, Wang and Amato hypothesized that adjustment would be associated with variables reflecting stressors, resources, and people's definitions of the divorce. Contrary to expectations, they found little evidence that stressors—including large declines in per capita income, along with losing friends, or moving—affected divorce adjustment, except among individuals who were not employed. The researchers did find, however, that adjustment was positively associated with income, dating someone steadily, remarriage, having favorable attitudes toward marital dissolution prior to divorce, and being the partner who initiated the divorce. In addition, older individuals showed some evidence of poorer adjustment than did younger individuals.

Hanson, McLanahan, and Thomson (1998) drew on data from both the 1987/88 (n = 13,008) and 1992-1994 (n = 10,008) waves of the National Survey of Families and Households, to examine the relationship over time between divorce and economic, parental, and community resources. Their results supported those from other studies, which showed that divorce has a seriously negative effect on the economic resources of mothers and children. The researchers also found, however, that reduced household income and standard of living experienced by divorced mothers was partially offset by increased support from family, friends, and community, and that the women regained some of their economic resources about 4-5 years following divorce. Although remarriage or cohabitation tended to reverse the negative consequences for women, as well as a mother's expectations for her children's education, they also tended to result in a decline of parental and community resources, according to the researchers. Finally, regarding the cause of divorce, the researchers found that certain differences in family resources, e.g., a lack of kinship and community ties, contributed to the risk of divorce while others, e.g., poor economic resources, did not.

The latter finding is consistent with that from a study by Dolan and Hoffman (1998), which showed that, although divorced women generally suffer a decline in income—which is affected by social, personal, and other variables—income or wealth is not necessarily implicated as a cause of divorce itself. According to Dolan and Hoffman, previous research suggested that women's reported causes of divorce varied depending on socioeconomic status (SES), even though SES had been routinely defined by husbands' income rather than their own. Furthermore, researchers had examined the importance of spousal career support as a determinant of divorce for women only among highly educated professional women. In Dolan and Hoffman's study, the researchers collected questionnaire data from 130 divorced women in southern California, to obtain retrospective accounts of factors that led to their divorce. The findings showed that, regardless of women's SES, the most frequently cited determinants of divorce were incompatibility and lack of emotional support. Women divorced fewer than 10 years rated lack of career support as a more important factor in their divorce than did women divorced longer.

Other researchers have confirmed that the economic impact of divorce on women is more severe than it is on men. Arditti (1997), for example, collected data from 212 divorced custodial mothers and 225 divorced noncustodial fathers in Virginia, to illustrate income dynamics both before and after divorce, as well as gender differences in income distribution. The findings confirmed trends uncovered in other studies, including that women's post-divorce economic decline appears to be more pronounced than men's.

Loew (1995) used a nationally representative sample from the March 1989 Current Population Survey to address factors that significantly affected the labor supply of divorcees 55 years of age and older, and whether these effects were different for divorced versus other unmarried women. A sample selection model of labor supply indicated that wages, education, pension wealth, and asset wealth were significant predictors of labor supply for both the divorced and the other unmarried women, although the strength of these effects differed. Medicaid coverage had a significant effect for the divorced women only. The results suggested that wages are a limited, yet important, resource for unmarried older women, especially for older divorcees.

Another study that investigated variables affecting income loss after divorce was that by Dixon and Rettig (1994). They used mail survey data from 209 single women in the Midwest to assess factors that predicted income adequacy for women two years after divorce. Based on multiple regression analyses, the researchers found that income adequacy for women after divorce was positively associated with total number of weekly work hours, personal resources of age and education, and perceptions of financial solvency.

Widowed Women

Research has shown that entrance into widowhood for women generally is associated with an economic decline. Hungerford (2001) examined changes in the economic well-being of elderly women at widowhood in both the U.S. and Germany, using longitudinal data from the U.S. Panel Study of Income Dynamics and the German Socioeconomic Panel. Economic well-being the year before the husband's death was compared with economic well-being the year after the husband's death. The results showed that, although the prevalence of poverty was different in the two countries, most widows in both countries experienced a decline in living standards, and many actually fell into poverty at widowhood. A fall in Social Security and pension income was the largest contributor to the fall in living standards. For Hungerford, the implications of the findings were that the retirement income system in both countries seemed to be adequate for married couples but appeared to fail for widows.

Several studies have investigated the relationship between income and changes in residential status and behaviors following women's entrance into widowhood. McGarry and Schoeni (2000) noted that the percentage of elderly widows in the U.S. living alone rose from 18 percent in 1940 to 62 percent in 1990, while the percentage of widows living with adult children declined from 59 percent to 20 percent during the same time periods. Data from the Integrated Public Use Microdata Series, 1940-1990, indicated that income growth, particularly increased Social Security benefits, was the single most important determinant of widows' living arrangements, accounting for nearly 50 percent of the increase in independent living. In contrast to earlier research, no evidence was found that the effect of income became stronger over the period. Changes in age, race, immigrant status, schooling, and completed fertility explained a relatively small share of the changes in living arrangements, according to the researchers.

Chevan (1995) reported that entrance into widowhood stimulates women to give up their most valuable asset, the home, and move within a relatively short period of time, though this behavior is mediated by a variety of intervening variables. The researcher used longitudinal data from the Panel Study of Income Dynamics to study residential mobility and test the hypothesis that entrance into widowhood stimulates residential mobility. The analysis showed that widowhood appears to be a triggering mechanism, with the peak of moving occurring in the first year of widowhood, preceded by a gradual rise in the probability of a move and followed by a gradual decline in that probability. Eventually, the majority of widowed persons move, but after 20 years of widowhood, about 40 percent are still in the house that they occupied when they were widowed. Chevan found that a variety of variables affect "holding on" and "letting go," including age at widowhood, health, duration of residence, educational attainment, excess space, income, race, homeownership, and single-family residence.

Kivett and Schwenk (1994) used the 1990 Consumer Expenditure Surveys to analyze the income and expenditures of widowed, divorced, and never-married women ages 65 years and older and living alone (n = 3,205). The results indicated that widows had less income and expenditures than divorced or never married women. The groups differed in the importance of various sources of income, although all relied on Social Security for 50 percent of their income. Schwenk also found differences in the women's spending patterns, but all allocated the largest share (about 40%) to housing.

Single, Never Married Women

Research findings over the years have shown a highly mixed picture for single, never married women, depending on education, occupation, parental status, and ethnic-racial background, among many other variables. A review of the literature reveals only a few prior studies of savings rates for single persons that provide limited estimates of consumption rates for one-person families. Some studies (Ruble, Patton & Nelson, 2000) have provided estimates by income and gender but did not adjust for age.

Various studies (Bianchi, 1995; Gonzalez, 2004; Zhan & Pandey, 2004) have focused only on single mothers, which generally have found them to occupy the lowest rungs on the socio-economic ladder. Many factors, however, have been shown to mediate the relationship between their income, wealth, and lifestyle.

Zhan and Pandey (2004) investigated the relationship between single mothers' education, prior work history, and current economic well-being. Through analysis of the 1993 Panel Study of Income Dynamics (PSID) data, they examined the effect of education on a sample of white and African American single mothers. Their results indicated that past work experience was a weak predictor of current economic well-being. Having education, particularly postsecondary education, on the other hand, significantly improved their economic status. The results challenge the "work-first" approach to alleviating poverty, and provide more support for designing policies to develop human capital, according to Zhan and Pandey.

Zhan and Sherraden (2003) examined the relationships in female-headed households of mothers' assets (home ownership and savings) to, respectively, the mothers' expectations of their children's educational achievement and actual educational outcomes. Analysis of data from the National Survey of Families and Households (NSFH) indicated that assets of single mothers were positively associated with the children's educational achievement, and that this relationship was partially mediated through expectations. Positive association of household income with child outcomes occurred mainly through mothers' assets. The results indicated that regression models that include income but not assets are underspecified, and that there is need for expansion of asset-based policies for poor women with children, according to the researchers.

According to Bauman (2002), recent changes to programs of income support for the poor have focused attention on how work requirements and incentives affect earnings and employment of single mothers, among other welfare recipients. The predominant way of thinking of these issues, at least in broader political discourse, assumes that obtaining work or improving wages are desirable goals for welfare recipients and their families, especially single mothers with children. However, recent research has begun to suggest that single parents and their families are not always better off in the labor force. This study, which used the 1991 and 1992 panels of the Survey of Income and Program Participation to examine welfare, work, and well-being in a broader context, found an apparent advantage of work over welfare for most households, but not for single-parent households. In addition, for the latter, material hardship was found to have strong effects on subsequent labor market participation and welfare use.

Among single women, financial strain is not necessarily related to being or not being employed, according to a study by Gyamfi, Brooks-Gunn and Jackson (2001). They analyzed data on 188 low-income, single, black mothers, including 93 former welfare recipients who were employed and 95 current welfare recipients who were not employed, to investigate financial strain, maternal depressive affect, and parenting stress. Their findings suggested that being employed did not reduce financial strain, as the two groups reported similar levels of strain. Regression analysis did indicate, however, that not being employed was associated with reporting higher levels of stress. Parenting stress also was associated with attaining less education, having boys, reporting more financial strain, and depressive affect. Correlates of material depressive affect were mother's education and financial strain, indicating that higher levels of depressive affect were related to more financial strain among unemployed mothers. Based on their study, the researchers concluded that, although employment was associated with better mental health for the single mothers, entry into the workforce was associated with stronger links between financial strain, parenting stress, and depressive affect for mothers leaving welfare.

Edin (2000) sought to learn the reasons single mothers give for not marrying, after noting that the choice to remain single would seem to perpetuate a cycle of low income, if not poverty, for these women and their children. For her study, Edin drew on qualitative interview data from 292 low-income African American and white single mothers in three U.S. cities, to explore the extent of and their reasons for nonmarriage. Based on inductive analysis, Edin identified five primary motivations for nonmarriage, several related to income. Most mothers agreed that potential marriage partners must earn significantly more than the minimum wage, but also emphasized the importance of stability of employment, source of earnings, and the effort men expended to find and keep their jobs. The mothers placed equal or greater emphasis on nonmonetary factors, such as how marriage may diminish or enhance respectability and limit their control over household decisions; their mistrust of men; and their fear of domestic violence. The researcher found that affordability, respectability, and control had greater salience for African American mothers, while trust and domestic violence had greater salience for white mothers.

Research also has shown that where single mothers live geographically affects their relative incomes, types of income, and assets. Lino (1996) used data from the 1990-1992 Consumer Expenditure Survey to examine the characteristics, income, and spending of 261 rural and 3,642 urban single-parent families. Analysis revealed that a significantly greater percentage of rural than urban single-parent families received alimony and child support, but a smaller percentage received public assistance. Before-tax income of rural families was significantly lower compared with urban families. Housing accounted for the largest share of total expenses for both groups. A significantly higher proportion of rural than urban single-parent families owned a home, with 29 percent of all rural single-parent families residing in a mobile home. In addition, Lino found that a significantly higher proportion of urban than rural single parents were never married, and that slightly more than 25 percent of single parents in both areas did not have a high school diploma.

Rubin and Nieswiadomy (1995) conducted a study of economic adjustment among single women and others upon their entry into full retirement, and its immediate impact on income and spending patterns. Based on analysis of cross-sectional data from the Bureau of Labor Statistics Consumer Expenditure Survey, 1984-1987, the researchers found that single females suffered the most substantial decline in postretirement income, but that this decline was not offset by concurrent expenditure decreases. This unsustainable dissaving rate after retirement posed a severe problem for single women, according to the researchers. Rubin and Nieswiadomy also found that, immediately after retirement, the participants showed significant increased proclivities to spend on transportation, health, entertainment, and trips; and that older retirees spent less than their younger counterparts for all expenditure categories except health insurance and gifts.

Dinkins (1995) used data from the 1992 Consumer Expenditure Survey to examine per capita income and expenditures for various types of households, including single-parent households, headed by baby boomers (n = 8,841) born between 1946 and 1964. Per capita comparisons were undertaken because average household size ranged from 1-4 people. The findings showed that single-parent households had significantly lower per capita income and expenditures than other households, and only 76% of income from earnings (whereas other baby-boomer households received 91% to 98% of their income from wages and salaries). Single-parent boomers also were more likely than others to receive public assistance income. According to the researchers, the results are useful to professionals who help families allocate their limited resources and to policymakers who evaluate the impact of different income sources used by families (especially single parents) to meet their everyday needs.

Studies of Women's Wealth and Demographic and Social Factors

Research has shown that women, irrespective of their marital status, experience income inequality relative to white men over the course of their careers, including in later life. In addition, demographic factors, such as race and age, and social variables, such as occupation and education, affect women's economic well-being, often in combination with marital status. In this section, I discuss several important studies that have examined these relationships for women in the United States over the past several decades.

According to Maume (2004), explanations of inequality usually diverge into two camps. The "persistent inequality perspective" suggests that all women and blacks face discriminatory barriers across their careers, while the "cohort explanation" contends that women and younger blacks are closer to wage parity with white men than are their older counterparts. Maume estimated minority wage gaps relative to white men for three cohorts of white women, black women, and black men, using longitudinal data from the Panel Study of Income Dynamics. The findings showed that, in the early years, younger women and minorities were significantly closer to wage parity with white men than were older cohorts. Yet, none of the cohorts gained ground on white men over their careers, and instead the majority of cohorts suffered significant wage erosion. Moreover, in a decomposition analysis of the average career wage, the majority of the gaps were attributable to unexplained factors (i.e., discrimination), rather than to compositional differences between white men and the other groups. Based on the study, Maume concluded that, on balance, the results were more consistent with the persistent inequality perspective than the cohort explanation.

Willson and Hardy (2002) pointed out that as women age their family and employment choices are linked to their financial security. Testing hypotheses that emphasized heterogeneity in women's experiences, particularly differences in income security by race, the researchers found that, while marriage in general offers women considerable financial protection—especially white women—their own employment is a key to their security. Most important, women's own employment reduced the rate at which their income security decayed as they entered old age. This factor was found to be most important for black women.

Vartanian and McNamara (2002) investigated the factors contributing to older women's economic well-being from a life course perspective, assessing the effects of both midlife characteristics and later life events on women between the ages of 66-

70, and 71-85. Using the 1968-1997 Panel Study of Income Dynamics, the researchers found that midlife characteristics such as income, workforce participation, and rural residence were strongly related to economic outcomes in old age. Late-life events and characteristics, however, also contributed significantly to economic outcomes even when midlife factors were incorporated into the analyses. In addition, the researchers found that both midlife and later life characteristics contributed to the persistence of poverty in old age, with many groups of poor women finding themselves in poverty for over 50 percent of their old age years.

Ozawa and Tseng (2000) conducted a study to estimate the net effect of gender and race on net worth in old age, and to investigate whether lifetime earnings and human capital variables had a differential effect on the level of net worth of elderly white and black people. The independent variables analyzed included race, lifetime earnings, and human capital (education, occupation, and labor force attachment). In addition, the researchers included the following demographic variables as controls: gender, marital status, age, and the number of children raised. The sample (n = 8,353), derived from the New Beneficiary Data System, included people who began receiving Old-Age-Survivors-and Disability Insurance (OASDI), Medicare, or both between 1980 and 1981, and who were interviewed in 1991. Among other things, the results showed significant differences in the net worth between women and men and between blacks and whites. Also, where lifetime earnings of white men did make a difference in net worth in old age, this variable made no difference in net worth for white women. The opposite was found to be true for black people: lifetime earnings did not affect the net worth of black men, but did have a positive effect on the net worth of black women.

Williamson and Rix (2000) noted that, despite recent economic gains for women, a substantial gender gap in financial security during old age remains, making women more dependent than men upon Social Security. Social Security plays an important role in providing for women's economic security. Based on analysis of the implications for women of several proposed changes in Social Security policy, including the call for the partial privatization of Social Security via the introduction of individual accounts, the researchers concluded that many of the proposals would have the effect of asking women, particularly low-income women, to shoulder a disproportionate share of the risks and burdens associated with the changes.

McLaughlin (1998) used data from the 1970-1990 Public Use Samples of the U.S. Census to examine differences in household income and poverty rates for metropolitan and nonmetropolitan women ages 55 years and older. Comparison of median incomes for women the same age across birth cohorts revealed that much of the improvement in women's economic well-being occurred because younger cohorts had higher incomes when they entered older ages. There was also evidence that incomes declined as the cohort aged. Nonmetro women had lower incomes and higher poverty rates than metro women in every comparison, even when demographic characteristics were controlled. While the metro/nonmetro income gap declined between 1970-1980, it increased between 1980-1990. The largest income gap occurred in 1991 for women ages 55-64.

Hogan and Perrucci (1998) noted that recent empirical research indicates that, from 1970-1990, the U.S. "gender gap" in employment income decreased while the racial gap for this variable increased. Interview data from a national sample of noninstitutionalized persons who retired and began receiving Social Security benefits, 1980/81, revealed a parallel pattern in retirement income. The gender gap was smaller in retirement than it was in employment, while the racial gap was greater.

Cross Cultural Studies

Ofstedal, Reidy and Knodel (2004) conducted a comprehensive analysis of older women, including gender differences in economic support and well-being, in eight countries in Southern and Eastern Asia: Bangladesh, Malaysia, Indonesia, Singapore, Thailand, Vietnam, Philippines, and Taiwan. The study focused on five multiple economic indicators, including (a) sources of income, (b) receipt of financial and material support, (c) income levels, (d) ownership of assets, and (e) subjective well-being. The findings showed that, whereas men tended to report higher levels of income than women, there was generally little gender difference in housing characteristics, asset ownership, or reports of subjective economic well-being between the sexes. In addition, the findings provided an important qualification of widely held views about both the globally disadvantaged position of older women and that, in some respects, unmarried women were economically advantaged compared to unmarried men. The latter finding was attributed, in part, to the fact that the women are more likely to be embedded in multigenerational households and receive both direct and indirect forms of support from family members.

In Great Britain, Gough (2001) examined factors that affected women's earnings during their working years and went on to affect their earnings in retirement. Using data from the Labour Force Survey, the researcher analyzed variations in pay between women and men. Based on the findings, Gough argued that factors relating to part-time working, career patterns, and types of occupation and employment contributed not only to keeping women's income lower than men's during their working life, but also to a reduced entitlement to benefits from occupational pension schemes after retirement. When the effects of women's greater longevity also were taken into account, a picture emerged of an increasing number of women facing poverty either in old age or in extreme old age. Gough argued that occupational pension schemes, most of which were constructed with the needs of the long-serving male breadwinner in mind, could be made more appropriate to the very different needs of female employees in a much more mobile and flexible pattern of employment.

Prus (2000) conducted a study in Canada to gauge the impact of gender and ethnicity/race on income inequality, using separate inequality analyses for male-family heads versus female-family heads and Canadian-born versus foreign-born family heads. The findings showed, among other things, that (a) the rate of income inequality decreased for all four groups in old age; and (b) there was somewhat less income inequality among male-headed families compared to their female counterparts during the traditional working years (i.e., up to age 60), indicating that gender played a role in the overall level of inequality. According to Prus, these findings suggest that, while some female-headed families were able to overcome income barriers, most were not. In old age, however, this trend was reversed; inequality was considerably higher among male-headed than female-headed families. This was largely because public pension programs, and not the labor market, become a key source of retirement income for female-headed families, while disparities in private sources of income were more common among families headed by older men.

Several cross cultural studies have examined the effect of having children, i.e., motherhood, on women's economic well-being. Davies, Joshi, and Peronaci (2000) claimed that children affect women's opportunities in the labor markets of most advanced countries in three ways, including an immediate effect on employment and longer-term effects on both earning power and pension coverage. To quantify these impacts on women's lifetime income in Britain, the researchers conducted a study that compared income data collected during the 1990s with estimates from 1980. They found that, although childrearing and employment had increasingly been combined over the period, the estimated loss of gross earnings associated with motherhood remained substantial. It continued to amount to around half potential earnings after childbirth for less qualified sections of the British female labor force, but had become smaller for highly qualified women. In general, the researchers felt the data showed how far motherhood jeopardizes financial security for women in old age, particularly for the least qualified.

According to Jones (1999), conventional wisdom holds that women and children in woman-led households are more economically disadvantaged and more vulnerable to impoverishment than their counterparts in other households. In this study, however, the researcher presented case examples from Bathurst, South Africa, to challenge this conclusion. The findings show that the women participants not only believed men were an economic liability, but also saw a multiplicity of economic advantages that accrued to women and children in households that excluded either a senior man or men. Many of these advantages are difficult to measure, according to Jones—or at least are not captured by conventional means of gathering economic data about households. Consequently, information derived from domestic economic surveys, as usually formulated, cannot alone be used to assess the relative economic status of different categories of households and those who compose them. Jones concluded that such data must be balanced by sound knowledge of the gendered nature of domestic economic relations and detailed attention to income flows within and between households.

Summary

Over the past several decades, many studies conducted in both America and other countries, using contemporary and historical data, have examined the relationship between women of every marital status and various economic-related variables, including income, tax transfers, savings, expenditures, employment, and approaches to managing money, among others. In addition, studies have been conducted on changes in economic variables brought about by discontinuities in marital status, such as from married to divorced or widowed, and changes in the life course, especially the entrance into old age.

In some of the studies, women have been the subjects of investigation in one country only, such as the United States, Canada or Iceland, while in other studies, women in two or more countries have been compared on a variety of socioeconomic indicators. Among the many studies conducted, mothers, both single and married, often have been the focus of investigation, with the focus on how the presence of children affects their economic lives. The literature also shows that researchers have been concerned with the transition of women into old age, and how that age status, along with other social and demographic factors, such as ethnicity, geographic region of residence, and prior work history, impact economic security and other economic variables during the "retirement" years.

Methodologically, the studies also have varied, in terms of the number of subjects investigated, the instruments used to measure economic and sociodemographic variables, the time frames studied, and the types of statistics used to analyze the data, among many other factors. Consequently, direct comparisons of findings from the studies are rendered difficult, if not impossible.

Nonetheless, the findings from the studies indicate, without question, that the marital status of women, considered either at a given point in time or dynamically—as in the change from married to widowed status—have a consequential impact on economic variables that affect women's lives, whether those variables be income earned, household net worth, security in retirement, or employment decisions, among many others.

One of the most consistent findings from the body of literature is that married women usually fare better economically then either never married, divorced, widowed, or separated women. This finding itself, however, is contradicted in some studies, showing that no single conclusion can be drawn based on women's marital status alone, without knowing other information about their lives that impact economic well-being, e.g., degree of education, socioeconomic status of origin, employment status of spouse, or number of children in the household, among other variables.

Another generally consistent finding from the body of research is that, as women enter old age, their economic status declines. This fact, however, is often the result of loss of spouse, and is apt to be especially severe when combined with loss of income from employment, owing to retirement, illness, or other factors.

A third generally consistent finding in the literature is that single women with children fare less well economically than any other type of woman, although this finding is mediated by other variables, such as socioeconomic status prior to motherhood, race, and familial support, among other factors.

While cross-cultural studies do not contradict research findings for women in the United States in any consistent or uniform way, they do sometimes reveal unusual results. For example, the study conducted by Jones (1999), in Bathurst, South

Africa, found that the women participants both believed men were an economic liability and saw many economic advantages for women and children in households that excluded a senior man. On the whole, however, such findings are anomalous, especially for modern industrial societies.

Given the variegated nature of the results of studies that relate marital status to economic variables in both the United States and countries around the world, it is clear that more research needs to be done. This is especially so during such uncertain times as we are living through in the U.S., marked by rapidly changing conditions of employment, Social Security, population age distribution, and household composition, among many other socioeconomic factors.

To add to our understanding about the complex nature of the relationship between marital status and economic security, especially among elderly women in the United States, I therefore conducted a unique empirical study using a large data set, which is the focus of the next two chapters. Specifically, in Chapter 3 I describe the method I used to conduct my study and in Chapter 4 I present the findings from my statistical analyses. The conclusions I draw about the impact of marital status on the economic well-being of women through the life course, based on all sources and types of data presented in this book, are discussed in Chapter 5.

Chapter 3
Method for Analyzing Data from the Rand Health and Retirement Study

In this book I draw conclusions about the impact of marital status on the economic well-being of women based mainly on analyses of data from two primary sources: empirical research by investigators from approximately the beginning of the 20th century to the present time (reviewed in Chapter 2), and the Rand Health and Retirement Study (HRS) 2002 advance data file, which was primarily funded by the National Institute on Aging (see Appendix 1 for a detailed description of the HRS). In addition, I conducted interviews with women in all the marital status groups during 2007. Findings from these conversations are included in the discussion and conclusions presented in the last chapter of the book.

In this chapter I discuss the method I used to derive the variables from the HRS for my analysis and present my unique hypotheses, based on the HRS data. In Chapter 4, I present findings from the data analysis and draw conclusions about the hypotheses tested.

In essence, the HRS, was designed to follow age-eligible individuals and their spouses as they moved through the life course from active worker to retirement. My overall sample included 10,389 female respondents, and was restricted to female respondents at least 50 years of age who were married, divorced, widowed, or never married. Women who were cohabitating were not included in my analysis.

Dependent and Independent Variables: Definitions and Measurement

The Dependent Variable: Economic Well-Being

According to the conceptualization of this study, the economic well-being of women is dependent on, or a function of, both marital status and other variables, discussed shortly below. Married women, for example, usually have access to their husband's income and often have income of their own, unlike women of other marital statuses; only widowed women may have access to Social Security survivor benefits; and older women, unlike their younger counterparts, may have access to Social Security retirement benefits. Based on facts such as these, one can appreciate why economic well-being is dependent on several major *sources* of income generally associated with and available to women of different marital statuses (see Table 1 of the Appendix). Measured in dollar amounts as continuous variables, the dimensions of economic well-being I analyzed for the study are defined as follows:

Total household income. As its name indicates, this variable refers to the total of all *income* of the household. It includes the following seven possible sources of income, for both women and, as applicable, their spouses: (1) the sum of individual earnings, (2) income from employer pension and annuity, (3) income from Social Security retirement, spouse, or widow benefits, (4) income from Social Security disability, (5) income from unemployment and worker's compensation, (6) income from other government transfers such as veteran benefits, welfare, and food stamps, and (7) income from alimony, insurance, pensions, and inheritance.

In this context, it should be noted that, because married women are more likely than widowed, divorced, or separated women to have access to income from sources generated by their husbands, I subtracted the contribution from their husbands for part of the analysis to obtain a clearer picture of women's income security. With regard to unmarried women in the sample, I assumed they were the sole contributors to the income in their respective households.

Total household wealth: An individual or family's "wealth" includes more than income alone, so I included other assets in the analysis of women's economic well-being. Specifically, I defined "total household wealth" as the sum of all the following wealth components minus all debt: (1) the value of the primary residence, (2) the net value of real estate that is not the primary residence, (3) the net value of all vehicles, (4) the net value of any business, (5) the net value of IRA and Koegh accounts, (6) the net value of checking, savings, or money market accounts, (7) the net value of CDs, government bonds, and T-bills, (8) the net value of bonds and bond funds, and (9) all other savings. The debt components of the "total household wealth" variable are as follows: (1) the value of all mortgages, (2) the value of other home loans, and (3) the value of other debt.

In addition to analyzing total household income and wealth, it was important to sort out sources of income both available for women of different marital statuses and that were affected by women's demographic and other background characteristics.

For these analyses, I identified the following seven income-related variables:

Individual earnings refers to the sum of the respondent's or spouse's (1) wage/salary income, (2) bonuses/overtime pay/commissions/tips, (3) second job or military reserve earnings, and (4) professional practice or trade income.

Individual income from employer pension and annuity refers to the sum of the respondent's or spouse's income from all pensions and annuities.

Individual income from Social Security retirement refers to the respondent's or spouse's income from Social Security retirement, spouse, or widow benefits.

Individual income from Social Security Disability or SSI refers to the respondent's or spouse's income from Social Security disability (SSDI) and Supplemental Security Income (SSI).

Individual income from other government transfers refers to the sum of the income from veteran's benefits, welfare, and food stamps.

Income from unemployment and worker's compensation refers to the respondent's or spouse's income from unemployment benefits or worker's compensation.

Spouse's income refers to the sum of all the above income variables for the respective spouses of the married women in the sample.

The Independent Variables

The independent variables I analyzed are those considered most important for understanding variations in the economic well-being of women, based on previous research. In addition to marital status, they include a woman's age, race/ethnicity, education, employment history, and the number of children she has had. Each of these is now briefly discussed, in turn:

Marital status: This variable is, of course, the primary independent variable in the study. It includes four categories: *married* (=1, n = 5,449), composed of respondents who were both "married" and "married, spouse absent;" *divorced* (= 2, n = 1,286), composed of respondents who were both "separated" and "divorced;" *widowed* (= 3, n = 3,346); and *never married* (=4, n = 308).

Age: For the study I constructed four age categories based on usual definitions, or "cut-off points," in the gerontological literature, which allow for examination of variation in women's income at different stages of the life course. They include women 50–64 years old (=1), who are often still in the labor force and earning wages or salaries; 65-74 years old (=2), who are generally labeled the "*young old*;" 75–84 years old (=3), who are generally labeled as "*old*;" and 85 years and older (=4), who are generally labeled the "*oldest old.*" For the analyses involving the age categories, I constructed each as a dummy variable, with 1=yes.

Race/Ethnicity: Based on the HRS, I collapsed the race/ethnicity variable into three categories: *White* (=1), *African American* (=2), and *Hispanic* (=3). Respondents were eliminated from the analyses who did not fall into one of these categories. They composed a minute fraction of the total sample.

For the analyses involving the race/ethnic categories, I constructed each as a dummy variable, with 1=yes.

Education: Education has been noted as a significant predictor of income for women across all marital statuses and is, therefore, important for this analysis. I measured education in total years (it is a categorical variable, including 1-16 years and 17 years and over). A categorical summary of years of education was constructed from the total years of education. This was recoded and indicates whether the respondent dropped out of high school, obtained a GED, graduated from high school, has some college, or is a college graduate.

Employment history: This variable is one of the strongest indicators of income security for women, who tend to have discontinuous work histories due to family and caregiving obligations. Employment history is related to income in that it predicts both present wage and salary income and future Social Security retirement benefits. For this study, I measured the four aspects of each respondent's employment history, including: (1) whether or not she was *currently working for pay* (1 = yes); (2) her *labor force status* (i.e., whether or not she was working full-time, working part-time, unemployed, partly retired, retired, disabled, or not in the labor force); (3) her *years of tenure at the longest reported job*; and (d) her *total years of* employment.

Number of children: Having children is, of course, importantly related to women's work history outside the home, and thus her sources of income, both in younger and later life. For the study, I simply summed the number of children for each respondent, including any stepchildren of either the respondent or her spouse.

Hypotheses

Based on the variables discussed above — as well as on both the life course, political economy, and feminist perspectives employed in the study (discussed in Chapter 1) and findings from empirical research (reviewed in Chapter 2), I formulated and tested the following hypotheses:

Hypothesis 1. Married women will have greater income security than women of other marital statuses.

Hypothesis 2. Married women will have greater total household wealth than women of other marital statuses.

Hypothesis 3. Married women will have greater income security as they age than women of other marital statuses.

Hypothesis 4. Widowed women will have less income security as they get older than women of other marital statuses.

Hypothesis 5. Older divorced women will have less income security than younger divorced women.

Hypothesis 6. Never married women will have a decrease in their income as they get older.

Hypothesis 7. For women of every marital status, there is a direct relationship between their years of education, employment history, and income security.

Hypothesis 8. For women of every marital status, minority women will have less income security than white women.

Hypothesis 9. For women of every marital status, there is a negative relationship between the number of children they have had and their income security.

The next chapter presents findings based on the HRS data and conclusions about the nine hypotheses stated above.

Chapter 4
Determinants of the Economic Well-Being of Women: Findings from the HRS Sample

In this chapter I present findings from my analyses of the 10,389 women in the Rand HRS data file. Specifically, the chapter is divided into three analytical sections, based on the statistical techniques used to analyze the data. In section one I describe the woman in terms of the independent and dependent variables (defined in Chapter 3), using the arithmetic mean, standard deviation, and percentages. In section two I present findings for the relationships between the independent and dependent variables, based on the Pearson correlation coefficient (Pearson "r"). In section three I present prediction models for both total household income and total household wealth, using multivariate regression techniques. The chapter concludes with a summary of results of the nine hypothesis tests and other major findings from the data analysis.

Descriptive Statistics

Demographic and Employment Characteristics

This section first describes the women in terms of their mean age, education, and number of children, and then by aspects of their employment history, for each respective marital status group. I analyzed employment history as an indicator of income, including Social Security retirement income or pension income, and measured it for the following variables: (1)

whether or not the respondent was currently working (1 = yes); (2) the length of the longest job ever held; job status, which indicates the status of the respondent's job history; and years worked, from self report (see Table 2).

Married Women. The 5,449 married women had a mean age of 65.7 years, an average education of 12.4 years (or just over a high school education), and a mean of 3.6 children—the highest number, as expected, for women in all marital status groups. About a third of the women were "currently" working for pay. On average, the longest time they spent working at a job was 15.3 years, and the total years they worked across their life course was just under 26 (i. e., 25.9 years).

Divorced Women. The 1,282 divorced women were exactly the same average age as the married women (65.7 years), and they had almost the same average education (12.2 years) and mean number of children (3.3). In addition, they worked the same mean number of years at a job (15.3). The divorced women, however, worked for a longer duration of their lives, on average, than the married women—30.0 years versus 25.9 years—which is likely indicative of divorced women being without a spouse.

Widowed Women. The 3,346 widowed women were the oldest in the sample, with an average age of 76.3 years. They had less education, on average, than both the married and divorced women, with 11.2 years of completed school, or a little less than a high school education. Their mean number of children was the same as the divorced women (3.3). In terms of employment history, they had the longest average job tenure

(18.0 years) but worked fewer years across their life course, 24.0, compared to women in the other marital status groups.

Never married women. The "single" women in the sample were younger than the widowed but older than the married and divorced women, with a mean age of 69.3 years. Their average education of 12.3 years was very similar to the married and divorced women, but they had fewer children, 1.9, than women in the other marital status groups. Considering their age, it is surprising, perhaps, that so many of these women—158 of the 308 (51.3%)—had children, even though they never married. As might be expected, however, their employment histories were "stronger" than those of the other women in the sample. On average, they worked 20.7 years at the longest job held and 32.5 years throughout their lives. These figures no doubt reflect the fact that they never had a spouse to depend on for income.

Total Household Income and Total Net Worth

This first part of this section describes the components of total household income and total net worth for women in all four marital status group combined (n = 10,389) (see Table 3 and Table 4, respectively), and the second part describes these income and wealth components for each respective marital status group (see Tables 5–8, respectively).

The components of the total household income variable are the following: (1) wage and salary income, (2) pension and annuity, (3) Social Security disability, (4) Social Security retirement, (5) unemployment and workers compensation, (6) other government transfers, (7) household capital income, and (8) other household income.

Total net worth is defined as "assets" minus "debt." The assets variable includes the following components: (1) primary residence, (2) other real estate, (3) business, (4) stocks, (5) bonds, (6) checking and savings accounts, (7) CDs, savings bonds and T-bills, (8) transportation, (9) total IRA, (10) other savings. The debt variable includes the following components: (1) total mortgage, (2) other loans, (3) other debt.

Total household income for all women. The mean total household income for all the women in the sample is $46,262. The largest portion of the total income is from household capital income, which has a mean value of $10,742. This variable is the sum of household business or farm income, self-employment earnings, business income, gross rent, dividend and interest income, and other asset income. It consists, therefore, of a large number of sources of income, and may explain why it constitutes a large proportion of the total household income—even larger than the $7,585 average wage and salary income of all married, divorce, widowed, and never married women combined.

The mean amount of Social Security retirement income is $5,300, while that of Social Security disability income is only $410. Pension and annuity income, however, has a mean value of $2,950, showing that women do not receive very much pension income. The women in the sample receive very little income from government transfers from veteran's benefits, welfare, and food stamps, with the mean amount being $215.

Total net worth for all women. The results show that the primary residence is the largest portion of wealth for all the women in the sample, with a mean value of $121,561. The mean value of stocks is $46,765, which is almost twice the value of checking and savings accounts (mean = $23,240). The average value of IRA and Keogh accounts, of $39,052, is more than the value of the checking and saving accounts, which is most likely due to the age of the women.

Other real estate and business compose relatively large shares of the wealth component. The mean value of "other real estate," i.e., apart from the primary residence, is $37,611, and that of business is $28,724—which is, again, more than the value of traditional investments such as checking and savings accounts. The mean value of transportation—a measure of all vehicles in the household—is $12,229, which is slightly less than the value of CDs, savings bonds, and T-bills ($12,317). The largest portion of the total debt component, which measures all debt of the household, is the mean value of the total mortgage, or $17,965. This figure reflects the fact that the primary residence, or home ownership, composes the largest portion of the wealth component.

Total household income by marital status. For this set of analyses, the variable "spouse's income" was computed as a sum of all income sources from the spouse, separate from the respondent, i.e., wage and salary income, income from pensions and annuities, Social Security income either from disability or retirement, income from unemployment or worker's compensation, and income from other government transfers. The spouse's income was added in the calculations for the married women because that component is a part of the total household income of married households. For divorced women, any alimony or other income they may have received is included in the *other household income* component. For the widowed women, incomes received from "Social Security spouse benefits" were computed in the Social Security retirement component of total household income.

As can be seen in Table 5, the results clearly show that married women have access to more income than women in the other marital status groups. The mean value of the total household income for married women is $64,682, which is more than twice the amount of the divorced women ($26,391) and the widowed women ($22,157), who have the least amount of household income, on average. The never married women have incomes close to that of the married women, at $51,438.

These data obviously show that having a spouse is a strong indicator of income security, as that component represents almost half of the total household income for the married women. The spouse's income component is $31,434 out of the total of $64,434, and the wage and salary income of the married women themselves is $9,091. Divorced women have the largest amount of wage and salary income at $12,720, which is slightly more than the never married women, who receive an average of $10,892 from wage and salary income. The widowed women receive the least amount of their own wage and salary income, which is a mere $2,857. With $8,512 income from Social Security, however, retirement revenue is the largest component of their total household income. The advanced age of the widowed women in the sample is the probable explanation of these results. They are also likely to be receiving Social Security widow's benefits, as well as their own Social Security retirement income.

The findings also interestingly show that the never married women receive more from pension and annuities than women in the other marital status groups, and that the revenue they receive from Social Security retirement income is second only to that of the widows, i.e., $5,349 and $4,820, respectively. These results may be related to the strong employment histories of the never married women (discussed above, see Table 2), because they are more likely to receive pension income and larger amounts of Social Security income based on those histories. In contrast, married and divorced women receive the least amounts of income from pensions and annuities, as well as from Social Security retirement.

For never married women, the largest component of total household income is from household capital income, which has an average value of $27,948—larger than that for any other marital status group. Total household capital income, as discussed above, is composed of several income sources, which may explain why it is such a large portion of the income for the never married women. They may have access both to more business and self-employment income and dividend and interest income than women who are or were ever married. In addition, never married women have had to rely solely on their own income, and are more likely to invest in their futures than women who have had a spouse to rely on. Total household income for the never married women is second to that of the married women, who have access to a spouse's income.

Total net worth by marital status. The results show that, overwhelmingly, married women are the most economically secure of women in all other marital status groups. The average total net worth for the households of the married women is $439,785, or more than three times the amount for single, divorced, and widowed women. Divorced women are second to the married women in total net worth, at $189,327, widowed women are third, at $177,797, and never married women are last, at $147,567, although their average income is greater than both divorced and widowed women.

For women in all marital status groups, the value of their primary residence or home ownership is the largest component of wealth. This is an indication of the importance of owning a home as a source of economic security for older women, regardless of their marital status. In this regard, married women have the most security, since their primary residence is valued, on average, at $161,227, more than twice that of all other marital status groups. The average value of the primary residence for divorced women is $80,350, for widowed women its $77,696, and for never married women it is $68,433.

The average value of other real estate for married women is $51,173, while for divorced women it is $47,112; for widowed women it is $14,814; and for never married women it is $5,664—almost ten times smaller than that of the married women. The average value of investments in business for the married women is $43,269, which is almost twice the amount for the divorced women, at $17,275; almost three times that of the widowed women, at $11,740; and almost ten times that of the never married women, at $3,722.

In keeping with this pattern, for married women investments in stocks, bonds, CDs, savings bonds, and T-bills are much greater a portion of their wealth than for the other groups. The average value of their stocks alone is $65,420. The widowed women have the next largest amount, at $29,540, followed by the never married women, at $25,380, and the divorced women, who have the least amount invested in stocks, at $17,659. Similarly, for married women the average values of CDs, savings bonds, and T-bills, at $15,164, is almost three times that of the divorced women, at $4,140, and larger than that also of both widows and never married women. These results indicate that married women have more liquid assets that can be invested in stocks, bonds, etc., which are more intangible, but result in future revenue as interest and dividend income.

The average value of the checking and savings accounts of the married women, at $29,963, is also larger than that of the other women. This is apparently because women in married households have more income and, therefore, are able to deposit more of that income in checking and savings accounts than women who are not married. In descending order, the average of checking and savings accounts of widowed women is $17,660, of never married women it is $13,135, and of divorced women it is $11,697.

The households of the married women also have more invested in IRA and Keogh accounts. The value of the accounts is $62,655, much larger than that of the households of the other marital status groups. Again, these results are an indication of the greater income that married women have access to, which can therefore be invested for the future. Never married women have more invested in IRA and Keogh accounts than either divorced or widowed women. Their IRA and Keogh accounts are valued at $23,282, compared to the accounts of the divorced women, $17,069, and the widowed women, whose IRA accounts are valued at $10,515. These results are related to the strong employment histories of the never married women, in that the duration of their years in paid employment is directly related to the amount they have invested in IRA and Keogh accounts. Moreover, the advanced age of the widowed women may account for their having the least amount in IRA and Keogh accounts, as they may already have began depleting the funds in those accounts.

As for the debt component of total net worth, the largest component of debt for women in all the marital status groups is the value of their total mortgage. Since the value of the primary residence of all the women analyzed is the largest component of wealth, these results are not surprising. The average total mortgage for the married women is the largest of the four marital status groups, but their homes are valued at much more than the homes of the other women. Although it is the largest amount, it is not proportionately as large as the value of their homes. Their primary residence is valued, on average, at $161,227, and their average total mortgage is valued at $25,294. This amount is not much larger than the average total mortgage of the divorced women, which is $17,188, but their primary residence is valued at $80,350, on average, almost half that of the married women. Similarly, the average total mortgage of the never married women is $14,378, but their primary residence is valued at $68,433, on average. Widowed women have the least amount of average total mortgage, $6,660, but their homes are valued at $77,696, on average. These results possibly can be explained by the age of the widows, who would have had a longer period of time to pay on their mortgages. It may be noted here, however, that women who are divorced or have never been married have more debt than women who are either married or divorced.

Percentages for components of total household income by marital status. The percentages shown in Table 7 compliment the findings shown Table 5, and discussed above, for *total household income by marital status.* These data show, for example, that the greatest source of income for married women is their spouse's income, since it represents 48.6% of the total household income. In contrast, the women's own wage and salary income composes 14.1% of the total household income. For divorced women, on the other hand, the results show that their own wage and salary income composes the largest percentage of their total household income, at 47%. For the never married women, their own wage and salary income, at 21.2%, is of more importance than for either the married or widowed women, but their household capital income composes the largest percentage of their total household income. Widowed women depend less on their own wage and salary income, which is 12.9% of their total income, than do women in the other marital status groups. Not surprisingly, the largest component of income for the widowed women is from Social Security retirement, which comprises 38.4% of their total household income. Social Security retirement is 15.1% of the total income for divorced women, 9.4% for the never married women, and just 5.7% of the income of the married women. This is a function of the advanced age of the widowed women, and indicates that they are more likely than women in the other marital status groups to receive Social Security income in the form of widow's benefits. Widowed women are also more likely than the other women to receive pension income, due to their age, as it is a larger portion of their total household income.

As for household capital income, the findings show that never married women receive the most from this source, 54.3%, compared to women in the other marital status groups. As discussed earlier above, the large number of sources within this component may explain the high percentage. These findings demonstrate that women who have never had a spouse to rely on may be more apt to invest in sources that will generate income in the future.

Percentages for components of household assets by marital status. The percentages shown in Table 8 compliment the findings shown in Table 6, and discussed above, for *total household assets by marital status.* These results show that, overall, home ownership is the largest proportion of wealth or assets for all marital status groups. The value of the primary residence is 34.2% of the household assets for the married households, 22.4% of all household assets for the divorced women, 41.7% of the household assets for the widowed women, and 41.1% of the household assets for the never married women. This outcome clearly signifies that home ownership is a good indicator of wealth, and that owning a home has a huge impact on income security.

For divorced women, the second largest portion of total assets is the value of other real estate, i.e., real estate that is not the primary residence, at 22.4%. This component is 10.9% of the total assets for the married women, 7.9% of the assets for the widowed women, and merely 3.4% of the assets for the never married women. It is difficult to explain this finding. It may be that the divorced women in the sample invested in other real estate as a means to generate income.

Next to owning a home, owning stocks is a large percentage of the total assets for widowed women (15.8%). The numbers are similar for the never married women (15.4%), and the married women (14%). Owning stocks is not as large an asset for the divorced women (8.4%), who, as discussed above, apparently have invested more in real estate.

Checking and savings accounts compose a larger percentage (9.5%) of the total assets for widowed women than for any other marital status group. Their percentage compares with 8% for the never married women, 6.3% for the married women, and 5.7% for the divorced women. Widowed women, however, have less invested in IRA and Keogh accounts than women in the other marital status groups. This may be an indication of their advanced age, in that they have their Social Security retirement income in checking and savings, which makes that income accessible. The IRA component of assets accounts for a larger percentage of the assets of the never married women (14.1%) compared to the married women (13.2%), the divorced women (8.1%), and the widowed women (5.6%). Moreover, for the never married, owning CDs, savings bonds, and T-bills constitutes a larger percentage of their assets than for the other groups, with that component comprising 7.2% of the assets of never married women, 5.8% for the widowed women, 3.2% for the married women, and only 1.9% for the divorced women. These results, again, indicate that never married women may be more likely to invest in their future than women who are or have been married.

Relationships Between Characteristics of the Women And Their Household Income and Wealth

In this section, I report findings for a series of analyses using the Pearson correlation coefficient (Pearson "r") that relate the demographic and employment characteristics of women in the four marital status group to (1) their total household income, (2) their total household wealth, and (3) individual indicators of these household variables. Findings for these analyses are shown in Tables 9 through 17. As can be seen, many of the coefficients are statistically significant, although their magnitudes often are small. These relationships are, nonetheless, of value for understanding the economic well-being of women, and constitute the focus of the ensuing discussion.

Women's Characteristics and Total Income and Wealth

As shown in Table 9, for each marital status group education is positively related to total household income. For married women, divorced women, and widowed women the results are somewhat stronger than they are for the never married women. The relationship between education and wealth varies across the marital status groups, with that for the married women, the widowed women, and the never married women several times stronger than for the divorced women.

The age of the women is shown to be related to their income but not to their wealth. As married women advance in age, their income decreases, as shown by the negative relationship across all the age categories for married women. For divorced women 50-64 years who still may be in the paid work force, the result shows a positive relationship with age. This relationship is negative, however, for the older age groups, which is not surprising since income tends to decrease for all individuals as they reach retirement age.

For the race/ethnicity categories, the results show a weak relationship to both total household income and wealth, but the relationships are negative and statistically significant in several instances. African American married women tend to have both less income and wealth than white married women.

Number of children is both negatively related to the incomes of all the women regardless of marital status. Having children is negatively associated with the wealth of both the married and widowed women, and the strength of this relationship is identical for both groups. It may be that the total net worth of these women is more dependent on their having some income than it is for the divorced and never married women. Number of children is not statistically significant for the wealth of the divorced women or the never married women.

In terms of the employment histories of the women in the sample, the relationships were, again, quite weak, but they were positively related to income. The relationship is stronger for those who are married, divorced and widowed than for never married women. Whether or not these women are currently working for pay is not related to wealth across all the marital status groups.

Job tenure is directly and weakly related to the income of the married, the divorced, and the widowed women in the sample. Surprisingly, the length of time the never married were employed at a job is not related to their income. It is, however, related to their wealth, somewhat more strongly than for the married women, the divorced women, and the widowed women.

The total years these women have ever worked is both positively and significantly related to the income and wealth of both the married women and the widowed women, but only to the income of the divorced women and only to the wealth of the never married women. The results for the never married women consistently differ from those of the other marital status groups, and continue to be unexpected. It may be that because these women have never had a spouse on whom to depend, their economic security (or insecurity) may be related entirely to different factors than for women who have had a spouse or currently have a spouse.

Women's Characteristics and Income by Marital Status

In this set of analyses, the characteristics of women in each marital status group, respectively, are related to the individual components of total household income.

Married Women. For the married women (see Table 10), the results show that educational attainment is statistically significant and positively but weakly related to their income from their own wages, pension, Social Security retirement, household capital income, other household income, and their spouse's income. These results are not surprising since educational attainment, generally speaking for the population as a whole, is directly related to income.

Those married women 50-64 years of age are more likely to still be in the work force than their older counterparts, and, therefore, this age category is directly related both to wage and salary income and is relatively strong. The results also show that the women 50-64 years old are the least likely to receive income from pensions, and Social Security retirement. In addition, the spouses of women who are in the work force are the most likely to be in the work force themselves, indicated by these results. Those married women who are 65–74 years of age, 75–84 years of age, and 85 years and older are less likely to be in the work force and more likely to receive income from pensions and Social Security retirement. This is indicated by the results shown here. There is a negative relationship between being in the age categories 65-74, 75-84, and over age 85 and income from wages, but a positive relationship between these age categories and income from Social Security retirement.

These results are consistent with the age at which individuals begin to receive income from Social Security retirement benefits. Moreover, the results show that as the women get older, their income from their spouse also decreases, suggesting that the spouse's income will also decrease as they age.

Race is shown to be both negative and weakly related to several of the income variables of the married women. Being an African American married woman is negatively associated with both income from a spouse, and income from Social Security retirement. Results for the Hispanic women are similar, in that the relationships are also negative for them in terms of their own wage and salary income, Social Security retirement, and spouse's income. Again, these women's minority status reflects the amount of income to which they have access.

The number of children the married women have had is negatively associated with their own wage and salary income, as well as income from their spouses. Obviously, having children has an affect on the income of a spouse. This result is somewhat counterintuitive, in that the expectation would be that the spouses would be working more. It may be that having children in the household reduces the commitment to the work force for a spouse as well as the women in the household.

Examining the employment histories of the married women, there is a positive relationship between currently working for pay and, respectively, both wage and salary income and spouse's income; and there is a negative relationship between currently working for pay and Social Security retirement income. Clearly, if an individual is still in the work force, he or she would be less likely to receive income from Social Security retirement. These results also indicate that, if a married woman is in the work force, her spouse is also more likely to be in the work force. Those who have had the longest job tenure are more likely to receive a pension and income from Social Security retirement, as shown by these results. Job tenure is positively related to wages, pension income, and Social Security retirement. This variable, however, is negatively associated with the spouse's income. The contribution of the wage and salary income from the married women, themselves, to the total household income may decrease the magnitude of the spouse's income.

Divorced Women. For the divorced women (see Table 11), the results, again, show that the effect of education on income is positive for several of the income components: wages, pension, and household capital income. These outcomes are consistent with what has been discussed above for married women. Those who are ages 50-64 are more likely to still be in the paid work force and, therefore, the relationship is positive for income from wages and salary and negative for income from pension and Social Security retirement income. Conversely, increased age is negatively associated with wages and positively associated with income from pensions and Social Security retirement.

Among divorced women the results for race and ethnicity diverge somewhat from findings for married women, in that fewer correlations are significant. Being African American is shown to have a weak, negative relationship with income from Social Security retirement. For Hispanic women the relationship is similar, as there is a negative relationship with earnings, pension income, and income from Social Security retirement. Although quite weak, these results do suggest that minority divorced women are likely to receive income from fewer sources than their white counterparts.

For the divorced women, number of children is significantly and negatively related to wage and salary income and positively related to both pension and Social Security disability income. Employment history is related to the sources of income, and the relationship is relatively stronger than what has been shown for the other variables discussed. Those who are currently working for pay are more likely to be receiving income from wages and salaries, demonstrated by the positive association; but they are less likely to be receiving income from pensions and Social Security retirement. Job tenure is also positively related to wage and salary income, as well as to income from pensions and Social Security retirement. Number of years in paid employment is positively related to income from wages, pensions, and Social Security income. These results suggest, therefore, that a strong employment history will ensure that divorced women will have access to a greater number of income sources, and also more income security, than those who have less of an attachment to the paid work force.

Widowed Women. For the widowed women (see Table 12), the findings are consistent with results for women in the other marital status groups. Educational attainment is statistically significant and positively related to income from wages, pension, Social Security retirement, household capital income, and other income. These results, again, suggest that educational attainment is an indicator of the number of sources of income to which these women have access.

For the age categories of the widowed women and their relationships to the components of income, some differences are worth noting. There is a positive relationship between wages and, respectively, age categories 50-64 and 65-74. These results diverge from what was found for the married and divorced women. It may be that widowed women will be in the paid work force after the age of retirement in order to stay out of poverty. The results for the older age categories are consistent with previous findings. There is a negative relationship for women ages 75-84 and 85 and older and income from wages. Looking at the results for pension income, there is, again, some inconsistency with findings for married and divorced women. Although there is a negative relationship between pension income and women aged 50-64—which means those still in the paid work force will be less likely to receive income from pension—the relationship is also negative for those 85 and older. It may be that the advanced age of these widows explains this finding, i.e., as they get older, the income they receive form pensions begins to decrease.

The race/ethnicity of the widowed women is negatively related to income from pensions for those who are either African American or Hispanic and to Social Security retirement; but these race/ethnic categories are positively related to income from Social Security disability. These findings indicate that older widowed minority women may be more likely to need income assistance for disabilities than their white counterparts.

For the widowed women, number of children is not statistically significant related to their wage and salary income, which is inconsistent with the findings for the married and divorced women. There is a significant negative relationship with income from pensions and Social Security retirement. The results of the employment history variables for the widowed women, however, are similar to those for the married and divorced women. Those who are currently working are not likely to be receiving income from Social Security disability or retirement, and are more likely to be receiving income from wages. Job tenure is positively related to pension income and Social Security retirement income, and is negatively associated with Social Security disability income. The more time spent employed at a particular job, the more likely that person will be eligible for income from pensions and Social Security retirement, and the less likely that person will be to receive income from Social Security disability. The duration of time in the paid work force is also related to income, as years worked is positively related to wages and pensions. Interestingly, number of years worked is not significantly related statistically to receiving income from Social Security retirement for the widowed women, although that variable includes income from Social Security widow benefits.

Never Married Women. For never married women (see Table 13), the results for educational attainment are similar to those of the other groups. There is a positive association with education and wages, income from pensions, and Social Security retirement.

Consistent with findings for the age categories of women in the other marital status groups, there is a positive relationship with wages if these women are ages 50-64, and a negative relationship if they are ages 65-74, 75-84, and 85 and older. As the age of these women increases, therefore, their wage and salary income decreases. Similarly, those 50-64 years old are less likely to receive income from Social Security retirement, as seen in the negative relationship for this age category, than those in the older age categories, as seen in the positive relationships. There is no relationship between the age of the never married women and their income from pensions.

The race/ethnicity categories of the never married women are not related to their income from wages and pensions, but they are related to their receiving income from Social Security disability income and retirement. White, never married women are less likely to receive Social Security disability than are African American never married women. Conversely, white, never married women are more likely to receive Social Security retirement income than African American never married women. There is a relationship between the status never married and government transfers, which was not found for women in the other marital status groups. There is a negative relationship for the white women in the sample, and a positive relationship for the African American women. The variable other government transfers reflects the sum of income from veteran's benefits, welfare, and food stamps. Never married African American women are more likely than women in the other race/ethnic groups to receive income from these sources. There is no relationship between the Hispanic, never married women and any of the income variables.

Number of children is not related to the sources of income for the never married women. Obviously, having children has had no effect on the labor force participation of never married women, since there has never been a spouse's income on which to rely. The results for their employment histories, therefore, diverge from those of the other groups. The one similarity is that those who are currently working for pay are more likely to receive income from wages, and are less likely to receive income from Social Security disability and retirement. Length of tenure at a job is not statistically significantly related to income from wages or pensions, but it is positively related to income from Social Security retirement. Duration of paid labor is positively related to wages, pension income, and Social Security retirement income, and negatively related to income from Social Security disability and income form other government transfers. Again, the relationship to income from other government transfers was not as strong, either positively or negatively, as for the other marital status groups. It seems likely that never married women may be more dependent on income from welfare and food stamps than the women who are married, divorced, and widowed.

Women's Characteristics and Wealth by Marital Status

Married Women. For married women (see Table 14), the results show that education is positively related to every wealth component, as it was related to the income variables. Having enough income to be able to invest in the intangible assets measured by these components is indicated by the positive relationships of education and, respectively, owning real estate; business; investing in stocks; bonds; amount in checking and savings accounts; having money in CD accounts, savings bonds, and T-bills; and the other items associated with wealth.

The age of the married women is related to several, but not all, of the wealth components. There is a negative relationship for those ages 50-64 and the value of stocks, bonds, checking and savings accounts, and CDs, savings bonds. There exists a positive relationship, however, between this age category and the value of both their vehicles and primary residences. For those ages 65-74, a positive relationship exists with both the value of their CDs and IRA and Keogh accounts; and there is a positive relationship between those ages 75-84 and 85 and older and the value of their CDs, savings bonds, and T-bills. On the other hand, the relationship is negative for these older age categories and the value of IRA and Keogh accounts.

Younger individuals may still be in the paid work force and have less income to invest in stocks, bonds, or CD accounts, but may be more likely to have a greater amount invested in their vehicles than those in the older age categories. The latter, of course, have had more time to accumulate investments, such as stocks and bonds.

For those ages 50-64, there is also a positive relationship with debt and the value of the total mortgage. Conversely, the debt and mortgage components are negatively associated with the older age categories. These results suggest that those in the older age categories have had more time to pay down their debts and mortgages than those in the younger age category.

The results for the race/ethnicity of the married women are interesting but not unanticipated. The relationship is positive across all asset components of total net worth for the white, married women in the sample. However, the relationship is negative for all components for the African American and Hispanic married women. These results indicate that the value of stocks, bonds, checking and savings accounts, CDs, vehicles, other savings, IRAs, and primary residence for the white married women is greater than for both the African American and Hispanic married women.

The number of children that the married women have had is negatively associated with the value of several of the wealth components. Having children to raise leaves less income available for investments.

Whether or not the married women are working for pay is positively associated with owning a business, value of vehicles, value of total mortgage, and other home loans. It is negatively associated, however, with the value of stocks, bonds, checking and savings accounts, CDs and savings bonds. If these married women are in the paid work force, they are probably in the younger age category (50-64 years), have not invested in those assets that are intangible and based mainly on future investments, and would be more likely to have more debt than those who are older.

Years worked at a job is positively related to investments in business, stocks, value of CDs, vehicles, IRAs, and primary residence. There is a negative association with debt and value of mortgage. The length of time worked at a job is related to income and, therefore, to having liquid assets available to invest in things such as stocks, bonds, and IRA accounts. This is related to the amount of income available to pay down debts, as well as to making it less likely to be in debt. The duration of time in the paid work force is surprisingly negatively associated with the value of stocks, bonds, and CDs, but it is positively related to the value of IRA and Keogh accounts, total mortgage, and other loans. These results are a reflection of the age of these individuals, and also may reflect their conscious decisions in terms of retirement planning and money management. These married individuals have more wealth than the unmarried women in the sample, and their greater wealth allows them to make these decisions.

Divorced Women. For divorced women (see Table 15), education is related to several wealth components but not to all of them, as was found for the married women. Years of completed education is positively related to the value of stocks, checking and saving accounts, CDs, vehicles, other savings, IRA and Keogh accounts, primary residence, debt, total mortgage, and other home loans. More education is related to income and asset accumulation. Therefore, the women with high educational attainment have more income available to invest in these components.

The age of the divorced women is not related to their wealth. The results show the respective relationships between the age categories and wealth components are weak. There is a relationship between those women 75–84 years of age and 85 and older and the value of CDs. The total value of vehicles is positively related to the 50-64 age category, but negatively related to both the 75-84 age category and the 85 years and older category. In terms of debt, those women 50-64 years old have more debt than those ages 75-84, and they also are more likely to have higher mortgages than those 75-84 and 85 and older.

The race/ethnicity categories of the divorced women are not related to their wealth. The results do show, however, that the white divorced women have greater wealth than both the African American and Hispanic divorced women. There is a positive association for the white women and the value of stocks, bonds, checking and savings accounts, CDs, savings bonds, and T-bills, vehicles, other savings, IRA accounts, and primary residence. The associations for the African American women are negative for the value of stocks, bonds, checking and savings, CDs, vehicles, other savings, IRA accounts, and primary residence. The results are similar for the Hispanic women, and negative in relation to the value of stocks, checking and savings accounts, CDs, vehicles, and primary residence. Although these relationships are weak, the findings suggest that minority divorced women have less wealth than their white counterparts.

Number of children is not strongly related to the wealth of the divorced women, but is negatively related to the value of CDs, savings bonds, and T-bills and the value of the primary residence. Similarly, currently working is related to few of the components of wealth, namely, the value of vehicles, IRA accounts, primary residence, debt, mortgage, and other home loans. Whether or not the divorced women are currently working for pay is a weak predictor of wealth for these women, but these results suggest that those who are in the paid work force have greater wealth than those who are not. Furthermore, as regards employment background, their job status histories are not related to their total net worth; and the tenure of their longest job held, as well as duration in the paid labor force, are weakly related to their wealth. Job tenure is positively related to the value of stocks, checking and savings accounts, CDs, other savings, primary residence, and mortgage. Years worked is positively related to the value of checking and savings accounts, vehicles, IRA and primary residence. Having a strong employment history will not guarantee that divorced women will have income available to invest in these assets or to be able to make decisions that will allow them to have access to the components of wealth.

Widowed Women. For widowed women, (see Table 16), education is related to their wealth, and this relationship is stronger than it is for the divorced women. There is a positive relationship between education and all the wealth components for the widowed women. These findings suggest that education is related to income and, therefore, the more years of education completed, the more likely that widowed women will have income available to make decisions to invest in the assets examined in this book.

The age of the widowed women is related to several of the wealth components. For those ages 50–64, there is a positive relationship for the value of vehicles, IRA accounts, debt, and total mortgage; and there is a negative relationship for the value of stocks, checking and savings, CDs, and other savings. For those ages 65-74, the relationship is positive for the value of vehicles, other savings, IRAs, primary residence, debt, mortgage, and other home loans; and the relationship is negative for stocks, and CDs. The results for women in the older age categories look a bit different than for the women in the younger age categories. For this 75-84, there is a negative relationship with the value of stocks, bonds, vehicles, and mortgage; and there is a positive relationship with the value of CDs. For those 85 years and older, the relationship is positive for the value of stocks, bonds, checking and saving accounts, CDs; and the relationship is negative for vehicles, IRA accounts, primary residence, debt, total mortgage, and other home loans.

The results for the race/ethnicity categories of the widowed women are consistent with that found for married and divorced women. There is a positive relationship for the white divorced women and the value of other real estate, business, stocks, bonds, checking and savings accounts, CDs, vehicles, other savings, IRA and Keogh accounts, and primary residence; and there is a negative relationship for the value of total mortgage. The results suggest that the reality is different for minority widowed women. There is a negative relationship for the African American widowed women and the value of real estate, business, stocks, bonds, checking and savings accounts, CDs, vehicles, other savings, IRA and Keogh accounts, and primary residence. The results for the Hispanic widowed women are similar to those for the African American widows. A negative relationship exists for the value of stocks, checking and savings accounts, CDs, savings bonds, and t-bills, vehicles, and primary residence. These findings are consistent with those found for the minority married and divorced women. White widowed women have greater wealth than minority widowed women.

For the widowed women, number of children is negatively associated with several components, including the value of checking and saving accounts, CDs, vehicles, and primary residence. As was shown for the divorced and married women, having children is not as robustly related to wealth as it is to income. Number of children is related to employment and, therefore, is related to income. In terms of wealth, however, the relationship seems to involve the more tangible assets, such as checking and savings accounts, vehicles, and the value of the home. There is no relationship with the more intangible assets, such as stocks, bonds, and IRA accounts, which may require higher incomes.

The employment histories of the widowed women are, again, not very strongly related to their wealth. Whether they are currently working for pay is positively related to a few of the components of wealth, as is longest job tenure, and duration of years in the paid labor force. Those with stronger employment histories will have more income and will, therefore, be able to invest in the wealth components. Furthermore, if they are able to invest more in the value of a home, they will be more likely to have greater debt and a higher mortgage than those whose homes are worth less, as indicated by the positive association with the debt components.

Never married women. For never married women (see Table 17)—unlike for the other marital status groups—the analyses show very few statistically significant results. Level of education is positively related to the value of stocks, checking and savings accounts, vehicles, other savings, IRA accounts, and total mortgage. Although not a strong predictor of the wealth of the never married women, the results show that those with higher educational attainment are more likely to have more wealth. This finding is consistent with what has been shown for the women in the other marital status groups.

The age of the never married women is rarely related to indicators of wealth. There is a positive relationship for those ages 50-64 and the value of their mortgages. A very weak negative relationship is evident for the other age groups and total mortgage. These results suggest that, for the never married women, as age increases, the amount of debt owed on a mortgage decreases. Again, this is consistent with findings for women in the other marital status groups. The age of the married, divorced, and widowed women, however, is a stronger predictor of wealth, and related to many more of the components of wealth, than is the case for never married women.

The findings for the race/ethnicity categories of never married women are consistent with findings for other marital status groups. The results show that white never married women are more likely to have more economic assets than African American never married women. Also, there is a positive relationship between being white and the value of stocks, checking and savings accounts, CDs, vehicles, IRAs and Keogh accounts, primary residence, and total mortgage. The relationship for the African American women is negative for the value of stocks, checking and savings accounts, vehicles, IRA and Koegh accounts, and primary residence. For Hispanic never married women, no relationship exists with any of the wealth variables.

Number of children is not related to wealth for the never married women. Clearly, having children has not been shown to have an effect on the assets that never married women may or may not have accumulated. Currently working for pay is positively associated with the value of other business, vehicles, primary residence, total mortgage, and other home loans. These results suggest that those who are still in the paid work force will be more likely to invest in some of the components of wealth examined in this analysis. As expected, these results confirm the association between current employment, the value of the home, and the level of mortgage indebtedness.

Surprisingly, the results show that the employment histories of the never married women are weakly related to their overall wealth. There is no relationship between either job history or longest job tenure and the wealth of these women. The duration of the time spent in the work force is positively related to the value of stocks, checking and savings accounts, vehicles, IRA and Keogh accounts, primary residence, and total mortgage. Although the never married women have been shown to have the strongest employment histories compared to women in other marital status groups, this variable is not shown to be related to their wealth. This was also evident in the results found for the amount of wealth among the never married women, in that they had the least amount of wealth compared to those women who are married, divorced, or widowed. It may be that never having a spouse to depend on for income impacts the availability of income that is invested in assets.

Predicting Women's Total Income and Wealth From Their Background Characteristics

To explain variance in the sources of household income, I computed two ordinal least squares regression analyses. The results of the analysis predicting the total household income components (or sources of income) by the characteristics of the women across the four marital status groups are shown in Table 18. For the married women, the results show that level of completed education is a stronger predictor of income than for women in the other marital status groups. Specifically, for every year of completed education, their income increases by more than $4,000. Educational attainment also is the strongest predictor of income for married women. In this analysis, total household income does not include the income of the spouse; therefore, educational level has the greatest effect on the income of the women themselves.

Looking at the results for the age of the women, one sees that age is negatively associated with the incomes for the women across all the marital status groups, but it is statistically significant only for the married and widowed women. Also, age is a stronger predictor of the incomes of the married women compared to the widowed women. Overall, these results indicate that as individuals get older, their income is likely to decrease.

African American married women are at a greater economic disadvantage than both minority divorced and widowed women. Although this characteristic is negative across all the marital status groups, it has the greatest impact on the incomes of the married women. Race was not shown to be statistically significant for the never married women.

Examining the results of the employment histories of the women, one can see that the variable currently working for pay has a stronger impact on the incomes of the married women than the other groups, but it is the strongest predictor of the incomes of the divorced women, compared to their other characteristics. The additional income from married women will have an effect on the total household income of married households; for the divorced women who do not have a spouse to depend on, however, their current employment status is even more important. This is, again, indicated by the fact that job tenure has a greater effect on the incomes of the divorced women compared to the other groups. These findings suggest that the employment of the divorced women is the main predictor of their incomes.

The model for the never married women shows this category does not predict total household income. As for previous analyses, the never married women have consistently looked different than the women in the other marital status groups. In this context, it should be mentioned that the lack of statistical significance for the never married women may be explained, at least in part, by the size of the samples for the respective groups. As noted earlier above and in the tables in the Appendix, the sample size of the never married women is very small compared to the sample size of the other groups (i.e., 5,449 married women, 1,286 divorced women, 3,346 widowed women, and 308 never married women were analyzed for the study). When a sample size is large, the results of analyses are more likely to be statistically significant than when a sample size is small. Nonetheless, the analyses have revealed some very interesting findings for the never married women that are worthy of further research.

For the multivariate analyses just discussed for total household income, all the models have a relatively low R^2, with each model explaining less than 20% of the variance in total household income. The fact that the correlation coefficients are small, as discussed above, is an indication of these findings.

The results of the ordinary least squares regression analysis predicting total net worth (or wealth) by the characteristics of the women across the four marital status groups are shown in Table 19. Interestingly, the results show a pattern consistent with that of the analysis for total household income. The model for the never married women, however, is more robust, and does show some significant results. The race/ethnicity of the never married women has a stronger negative effect on their wealth than the other characteristics in the model, while their level of education has a relatively strong positive effect on their wealth.

Looking across the marital status groups, the level of completed education is the strongest predictor of the wealth of the married women, compared to the other groups. In addition, it is the strongest predictor of wealth within the characteristics of the married women. This result is consistent with the findings for their income. Educational attainment is shown to have a strong effect on the wealth of the widowed women as well. Thus, women with high educational attainment are more likely to have more income than those with fewer completed years of education. This human capital effect is reflected in the fact that the increase in income will allow these women to have more invested in the assets measured by the total net worth variable.

Consistent with the results for income, the race/ethnicity of the married women has a strong, negative impact on their wealth. This represents a much larger effect for the married women than for the other marital status groups. Again, the results indicate that African American married women are at a huge economic disadvantage compared with their white counterparts. For the never married women, race has the strongest effect on their wealth, net their other characteristics. These outcomes are a reflection of the disadvantage that minority women face in the labor market, resulting in less income and, therefore, less wealth.

Examining the results of the employment histories, one can see that currently working for pay has a negative impact on the wealth of the married women, but is not shown to be statistically significant for the women in the other marital status groups. This may be related to the age the married women would be if they were in the paid labor force. Therefore, they would have less opportunity to invest in any of the components of wealth. Longest job tenure has a stronger effect on the wealth of the divorced women, than for the women in the other groups, and is the strongest predictor of their wealth within the model. As discussed previously (see discussion above and Table 18), the employment histories seem to be a strong predictor for women who have been married but no longer have income from a spouse upon which to depend.

All the models have a relatively small R^2, although the model for the never married women explains 21% of the variance in their total net worth, and is more robust than the model predicting their income. These results diverge from what was shown for the model predicting the income of the never married women. The characteristics of the never married women, therefore, have a stronger impact on their wealth than on their income.

Summary and Conclusions

The goal of this chapter was to examine the effect that marital status has, both alone and in combination with other variables, on the economic well-being of women at least 50 years of age, Specifically, my analyses describe selected work-related (i.e., socioeconomic) and demographic variables that would possibly modify the impact of marital status on income and net worth, including the age of the women, their educational attainment, their work histories, and the number of children they have ever had. These factors affect the number of sources of income a women may have access to, regardless of marital status. Hypotheses regarding the effects of marital status, age differences, minority status, working experience, and number of children were set forth in Chapter 3. This section will discuss specific findings related to the hypotheses.

Investigating the first hypothesis, it was expected that married women would have greater income security than women of other marital statuses. Results from the analyses support this expectation. Apart from the effect of other demographic characteristics, married women have the largest amount of income and the greater number of sources of income, due to their having access to their spouse's income. In fact, descriptive results (see Table 7) show that income from the spouse composed over 48 percent of the total household income for the married women.

Related to this, the second hypothesis states that married women will have the greatest amount of wealth compared to the women in the other marital status groups. There is support for this hypothesis as well. Wealth is measured by total net worth (accumulated resources), and descriptive results (see Table 8) indicate that, across all the components of the total net worth variable, those values associated with the assets of the married women were greater than those of the other marital status groups.

Age is an indicator of economic well-being, in that as individuals age, their assets and income tend to decrease, which results in less economic security in older age. As the third hypothesis states, however, those women who are married will have greater income security as they age than those who are either widowed, divorced, or have never married. They will have access to their husband's income from Social Security and pensions, as well as their own. Results of the bivariate and multivariate analyses lend moderate support for this hypothesis. There is a positive correlation between income from wages of the women, themselves, and their spouse's income for the younger age women, who are most likely to be in the work force. The results also show, however, that there is a negative relationship between wages and spouse's income for older women, indicating that they will receive less income as they age.

A positive relationship between the older age categories and income from pensions and Social Security retirement income is consistent with the age at which individuals begin to receive income from these sources. Married women have access to their husband's pensions and Social Security, and possibly also to their own, which means this decrease will impact them less than women in the other marital status groups. The results of the multivariate analysis indicate that the age of the married women has the largest negative effect compared to women in the other marital status groups. The results, however, are not statistically significant for the divorced and never married women. On the one hand, the married women are more dependent on their spouse's income as they age, but on the other hand, the presence of a husband remains a source of income security that is missing for women in the other marital status groups.

The next three hypotheses are related to the income security of the unmarried women. They state, respectively, that widowed, divorced, and never married women will have less income security as they get older. There is support for these hypotheses as well. For the widowed women, results of the bivariate analyses show a negative association for several sources of income and increasing age. These women do, however, receive income from pensions. The divorced and never married women are not likely to receive pension income as they advance in age, suggesting that widowed women may be more likely to have access to the pension income from their deceased husbands. The implications of these findings are that, although widowed women will experience a fall in Social Security and pension income, the decline will not be as great as expected for divorced and never married older women.

The results for the foregoing analyses are consistent with findings from previous studies, which show that divorce has a serious negative effect on the resources of divorced women (Hanson, McLanahan, & Thompson, 1998; Morgan, 1991). Their wage and salary income declines as they age, but their income increases from Social Security retirement benefits. It appears, therefore, that one source of income will be replaced with another through the life course. Nevertheless, Social Security retirement income is usually less than wage and salary income, and thus the former does not fully compensate for the latter. Moreover, although the divorced women have the largest amount of income from wages and salaries compared to women in the other marital status groups, they receive less income from Social Security retirement than both widowed and never married women. The findings for the never married women are similar. Again, these findings indicate that one source of income will be replaced by another less substantive source through the life course. Consequently, these women will receive less income in older age.

One characteristic that may improve the economic outcomes for women is educational attainment. It is stated in the seventh hypothesis that, across all marital statuses, as years of education increase, income security will increase. There is strong support for this hypothesis. Results of the bivariate analyses indicate that years of education are statistically significant and positively related to both income and wealth for the women in all the marital status groups. In fact, education is a strong predictor of most sources of income and components of wealth for women regardless of marital status, which increases both income security and access to accumulated assets. Furthermore, the results of the multivariate analyses support the hypothesis. Completed years of education were shown to be a strong positive predictor of the incomes of the married, divorced, and widowed women, and a strong predictor of the wealth for women in every marital status group.

Educational attainment, however, may not mediate the economic disadvantage minority women may have. They tend to earn lower wages, have fewer full time jobs, have less access to pension plans, and receive lower income from Social Security retirement. Thus hypothesis eight states that, across all marital statuses, minority women will have the least amount of income security. This hypothesis was supported by the results of both the bivariate and multivariate analyses. Regardless of marital status, both the African American and Hispanic women receive less income and have less accumulated wealth than their white counterparts. Furthermore, married minority women were not shown to be at an economic advantage, as was shown for the white married women. Results of the bivariate analysis did show a negative relationship for income from a spouse for both the African American and the Hispanic married women. The results of the multivariate analysis confirmed these findings.

Finally, the link between work and family, i.e., having children, is strong, causing women to have discontinuous work histories in response to family responsibilities, which results in less income. Hypothesis 9 states there is a negative relationship between having children and income security regardless of marital status. Outcomes of both the bivariate and multivariate analyses did not provide support for this hypothesis. Although the bivarate results did show a very weak negative relationship between income and wealth, the multivariate results did not show any relationship between number of children and income or wealth for the women in the sample. The implications of these findings will be discussed in detail in Chapter 5.

Chapter 5
Discussion and Conclusions

In this book, I analyzed the relationship between marital status and its economic consequences for women, especially those in the later stages of the life course, including how this relationship is modified by selected demographic and background characteristics, such as age, educational status, and ethnicity. In addition to a meta-analysis of prior literature, I conducted a unique statistical analysis of data from the Rand Health and Retirement Study (HRS) 2002 advance data file, to test hypotheses I formulated, derived from both the prior research and assumptions of the Life Course, Feminist, and Political Economy of Aging perspectives. For my empirical analysis, I used a sample of women age 50 and older and who were married, divorced, widowed, and never married.

In addition, during the winter of 2006, I conducted interviews with several women, between 45 and 80 years of age, including five who were married, three who were widowed, two who were divorced, and one who had never been married. The purpose of the interviews was to add an anecdotal dimension to the discussion and conclusions based on the findings from the empirical literature and my data analysis. In the remainder of this chapter, I present information from the interviews where appropriate.

A major premise of this book is that differences in the economic well-being of married and unmarried women are directly related to their income sources, with married women having the advantage because of their access to their spouse's income sources. I expected marital status, therefore, to have a substantial impact on the incomes and assets women I analyzed in the HRS data set. My expectation was based largely on previous research studies, which consistently have found that, at virtually every stage of the life course, women as a group earn less than men, and married women fare better than their unmarried counterparts.

In the remainder of this chapter, I will review and discuss the specific findings from the analyses conducted, as well as revisit the role of social policy, introduced in Chapter 1. The role of social policy for addressing the needs of women at economic risk cannot be overlooked. This is especially true in the 21st century, with more women living longer than ever before in history—and without spouses—because of steadily increasing rates of both widowhood and divorce. I will conclude the chapter with a brief discussion of the limitations of my research and the study's contributions to the existing literature.

As regards my analysis of the HRS advance data file, I hypothesized that married compared to unmarried women generally would have access to more sources of income and, therefore, have the greatest economic security. My findings supported this expectation. Consistent with findings from previous studies (DeViney & Solomon, 1995; Hirschl, Altobelli, & Rank, 2003; Willson & Hardy, 2002), I found that married women have access to their spouse's income as well as to their own, which is key to their security. More specifically, the additional income from the spouse has a huge impact on the total household income of the married women. In this context, it should be mentioned that some observers view the spouse's income as a source of both economic dependency for the married women and of family inequality, which is critical to women's economic vulnerability outside of marriage (Bianchi, Casper, & Peltola, 1999). The findings from my empirical analysis can support this premise. Those women who were divorced, widowed, and never married had considerably less income than their married counterparts.

Marriage does not necessarily protect women, however, from economic insecurity. It can vary depending on the employment status and history of the spouse, among other variables. For some women, these factors will result in financial difficulties. One of the women I interviewed, for example, is living this reality. Her spouse has been in and out of the work force due to recurring illness, and for several years has been self-employed. His wage and salary income has been inconsistent, and oftentimes has been nonexistent. He is presently receiving benefits from Social Security Disability and does not have any pension income. On the other hand, his wife, my interviewee, has been in the labor force most of her adult life, and has created her own security through her strong work history. This couple's combined assets also enhance her security. She has invested in a 401k account, for example, and the couple owns a home.

Economic security and well-being also are measured by net worth, which I have defined earlier as the value of assets minus debt. Greater net worth allows a family to maintain its standard of living when income falls because of job loss, health problems, family changes, or other reasons. Based on my data analyses, I found that the assets of married women are substantially greater than the assets of divorced, widowed, and never married women, in keeping with previous research (Goetting, et al., 1995; Wilmoth & Koso, 2002). The absence of a spouse, therefore, results in a large disparity between the economic security of married and unmarried women.

One of the unique features of my analysis of the HRS advance data file was the inclusion of never married women, who were compared on the same characteristics to women in the other marital status groups. Although the sample size of the never married group was relatively small compared to the other groups, some interesting findings are worth noting. One might expect the income and assets of never married and married women to be comparable, since the lack of both a spouse and dependency among the former group would result in their drive for greater economic security. This expectation was not supported, however, by my research. Although I found the never married women to have stronger employment histories than women in the other marital status groups, and their incomes were only slightly lower than incomes of the married households, their accumulated assets or wealth were significantly lower than for the married women. This was the case for never married women even though I found that their income from Social Security retirement benefits and pensions and annuities were much larger than for married women. The absence of a spouse and, therefore, the lack of income from a spouse throughout the life course, did not allow for the accumulation of assets among women who never married that was available to women who were married or had been married.

In addition to the unique empirical research I conducted, another feature of my analysis not found in prior work on this topic is the use of a multi-theoretical framework as the conceptual underpinning. As discussed in Chapter 1, my conceptual framework, or model, is derived from a combination of the Life Course, Feminist, and Political Economy of Aging perspectives. While the findings presented in this book can be understood within the context of each of these respective frameworks, I believe that a more satisfactory understanding is obtained through a synergistic approach that combines elements of each of these perspectives.

In previous chapters of this book I have presented findings from both prior research and my analyses of the HRS data file that incorporate women's background and demographic characteristics, including age, race, educational attainment, number of children, and employment history, among others. Age, for example, was found to affect the income of women regardless of marital status. Not surprisingly, my findings were consistent with the notion that the economic status of women decreases with age (Street & Wilmoth, 1999; Vartanain & McNamara, 2002; Williamson & Rix, 2000). Specifically, I found a negative association between age and income for women in all the marital status groups. For the married women, this leads me to conclude, along with others (Bianchi, Casper, & Peltola, 1999) that dependency on their husband's income increases as they reach advanced age. I further conclude, however, that the decrease in income with age impacts married women the least, because their average total household income is much larger than it is for divorced, widowed, and never married women.

I also found that, as the women grew older, the income sources available to them changed. For some of the women, the change resulted in a shift from wage and salary income to more government funded sources. The widowed women received more income from pensions as they aged than both the divorced and never married women. I concluded from this finding that widowed women may be likely to have access to the pension income from their deceased husbands. Widows will experience a decrease in their own Social Security and pension income, therefore, but this decline will not be as great as that found for divorced and never married older women.

Once again, however, this outcome depends on whether the spouse received pension income. For some widows, the lack of pension income from their husbands, coupled with low income from Social Security retirement benefits, has resulted in their entering the labor force much later in life. Several widows I spoke with entered the work force at age 70 or later! They did so to secure adequate income to meet their needs. Another respondent said she took a secretarial position when she was 60 years old—a time when most people would begin to think about leaving the work force. As we continued our conversation, she revealed to me that her husband died at the age of 47, and left her widowed at the age of 45, with five children to care for. Since he was self-employed, the income she received as a widow was lower than it would have been if he had been employed by another, and was not vested in a pension. She decided to go to work at an older age, therefore, in order to secure some pension benefits of her own.

Two other widowed women I interviewed revealed similar stories. Both were in their 80s and in the work force, to supplement their incomes during their later years. One of the women was 80 years old and worked part-time at a retail establishment. Her husband died at a young age, and had not worked long enough to secure a pension. The amount of monthly Social Security benefits she received was low, furthermore, because her husband's wage and salary income were low when he was in the paid work force. She raised her children, found that she was very financially insecure, and needed to enter the work force to supplement her monthly income from Social Security.

For divorced women, this book has presented evidence from both previous research (Hanson, McLanahan, & Thompson, 1998; Morgan, 1991) and my analyses of the HRS data file, that divorce has a serious negative effect on the resources of women as they grew older. While my data analysis showed that divorced women, compared to married, widowed, and never married women, had the largest amount of income from wages and salaries, I also found that they received the least amount of income from both Social Security Retirement and pensions. This finding leads to the conclusion that one source of income is replaced with another, as one moves through the life course.

In particular, most formerly married women experience a substantial decrease in their economic well-being after they divorce. Several women I interviewed reported the nature of some of these changes. They had owned their homes while married, but had to give up home ownership when the divorce became final. One women, age 45, had been an aspiring artist with a studio in the home she owned with her husband. She found she could not manage the finances of home ownership alone, so she moved into an apartment with her two children and took a job at a mortgage company. Interestingly, she informed me that several women who have come into her office are surprised when they discover they cannot afford to keep their homes.

Although divorce and widowhood generally adversely affect the economic well-being of women, especially during later stages of the life course, I identified several factors in this book that can offset or ameliorate the negative consequences. One such factor, years of education, a form of human capital, has a positive impact on the amount of income for women in all marital status groups. Higher educational attainment also is directly and positively related to the wealth components. Thus, higher education generally results in greater income security for women, irrespective of their marital status. However, I found the impact of education on the incomes and assets of the married women to be greater than for women in the other marital status groups. It seems that married women are able to invest more heavily in their education. This human capital effect may also allow married women to be more selective in their employment choices compared to unmarried women. Women who are divorced or widowed may have less opportunity to be selective and feel a greater sense of urgency to accept whatever employment is available. Highly educated women also tend to marry highly educated men, which represents another advantage for married women.

For never married women, however, the research results show that educational attainment has a great impact on their economic security. In my analysis of the HRS data file, I found that years of education has a significant, positive impact on the net worth of never married women. The situation of one of the women I interviewed exemplifies this finding. She is a highly educated, professional woman with two, young, adult children. Occupationally, she both runs a successful medical practice and owns a retail business that sells a product she developed. As she reaches her later years, she will be financially secure. Accumulating assets seem to be dependent on the educational attainment of the never married.

Race also has been shown to mediate the relationship between marital status and economic well-being among women. While marriage enhances the lifetime probability of affluence, for example, this advantage varies sharply by race. Both prior research and my HRS data file analyses have shown that minority women are at a clear disadvantage, regardless of marital status or educational attainment. My data analysis showed that having a spouse did not prove to be an advantage for the minority women. While the labor force participation rates of black women have always been higher than for women in any other racial/ethnic group, they also have experienced the most employment instability (Willson, 2003). In addition, minority women (as well as men) earn lower wages and have both fewer full time jobs and less access to pension plans than their white counterparts. In addition, although minorities depend on Social Security for most of their old age income, they receive much lower benefits than white recipients, because Social Security benefits are based on lifetime earnings (Street & Wilmoth, 2001). Minority women also are less likely to qualify for spousal benefits (Willson, 2003).

In this context, the concepts of cumulative advantage/disadvantage and status maintenance are especially relevant. The former posits that some effects of inequalities are magnified with the passage of time (Crystal & Shea, 1990), and the latter implies that inequality in old age represents a continued effect of inequalities generated earlier in the life course, such as in the labor market (Henretta & Campbell, 1976). My findings, for the minority women in the HRS data file, demonstrate both of these concepts. Minority women, therefore, are relatively disadvantaged throughout the life course (O'Rand, 1996), a fact that is especially significant if they are unmarried.

The life course theoretical framework allows one to examine the trajectories and transitions an individual experiences through the life span (Elder, 1985). Within this framework, the emphasis is on the links between early and late events, and the social and economic contexts within which trajectories develop (George, 1993). Hence, it is from the life course perspective that I have examined the impact of opportunity structures available to women at different stages of their lives. Analyzing women at different ages has increased our understanding of the mechanisms in place that impact the economic well-being of women as they age. As shown in this book, women's economic security generally deceases with age, and the decrease is exacerbated for unmarried women.

Income inequality is highest for women in the oldest age categories, and individuals in the bottom quintile of income distribution are predominantly female. The outcomes for these individuals have been shaped, however, by the historical times and societal mechanisms in place (Elder, 1985). The older women I empirically analyzed were born between 1917 and 1937 and at retirement age by or before the time of the study. They had made decisions across their life course consistent with societal norms, e.g., they were more likely to marry and less likely to be in the paid labor force after marriage (O'Rand & Henretta, 1999).

According to the literature, wealth accumulation is another important aspect of the economic well-being of all women, especially the elderly. Home ownership is a particularly essential component of assets, and is a significant contributor to the total net worth of the elderly (O'Rand & Henretta, 1999). In my data analysis, I found that for all women, regardless of marital status, the value of the primary residence comprised the largest portion of their wealth components. The difference across the marital status groups was large, however, with home values of the married women considerably greater than those of the other women. In fact, the homes of the never married women had the least value. I found this result to be somewhat surprising, since the never married women I analyzed had total household incomes very similar to those of the married households. This perpetual inequality in the married households is due primarily to the presence of a male spouse, demonstrated by the amount of the wage and salary income of the married women themselves.

With such relatively low incomes, many married women are, therefore, at risk of impoverishment should they lose their spouses to either death or divorce.

One can recognize the structural influences demonstrated by these research findings by employing the political economy of aging theoretical perspective in conjunction with the life course perspective. This dual perspective highlights the relevance of social struggles embedded in power relations, and the political and economic forces that account for the distribution of societal resources, which either maintain or increase inequality based on class, race, or gender (Estes et al., 1996). According to this perspective, the structure of the sources of income is grounded in a conceptualization of family status that is both permanent and based on a traditional family model, with a male breadwinner and a dependent family caregiver. Central to this discussion are concepts examined throughout this book, especially that women's economic well-being is dependent on the sources of income available to them, which are, in turn, associated with different marital statuses. My findings support the argument that the income security of older women is strongly affected by the state's role in sustaining the subordination of women. Thus, women's dependence is reinforced through a spousal wage relationship.

In addition to the above-mentioned theoretical perspectives, the feminist perspective emphasizes the different ways men and women experience aging, and how the differences are related to the distribution of resources. The socially constructed nature of gender affects the life chances of individuals and their access to financial resources in old age (Moen, 1996). My research is embedded in this framework. Hence, women's late-life economic status is affected by a complex combination of decisions and events experienced across their life course, which are influenced by the gendered nature of societal structures.

Women who exit and enter the work force because of family obligations are at a disadvantage in their later years, as a direct result of the way Social Security and pension income is structured. Social Security is based on the wage and salary income an individual receives throughout his or her working life. Women who left the work force when their children were born, and worked part time because of family obligations, receive low Social Security benefits. They also are less likely to be eligible for pension income when they retire. Several of the women I interviewed, who are not yet at retirement age, discussed these factors. Although they are still in the work force, they will not be eligible for pension income when they do retire, and they sometimes work two or three part-time jobs, to be able to secure enough income to maintain their households. These women are married, have at least two years of college education, and are professionals. One of them, who has been employed in the same workplace for the past 30 years, will loose several hundred dollars in monthly pension income because her job description changed during the years she worked part-time. Thus, the pension model in place and the manner in which Social Security retirement benefits are structured do not effectively work for women or families in the U.S. today.

Summary

The findings presented in this book have shown that marital status directly affects the economic well-being of women in later life, and contributes to our understanding of the existing mechanisms that influence the relative risk of poverty older women experience. This risk is directly related both to the different sources of income and wealth associated with each marital status and the role of social policy in addressing these differences.

A central policy issue, for example, is how policy can accommodate women whose family commitments lead to lower early labor force participation that affects their individual retirement income and then later may became divorced or widowed. While changes in social policy are beginning to acknowledge the implications for retirement income of the changed family status of older women, this situation continues to be problematic.

Over the past several decades in America, there has been a great increase in the labor force participation of women, as well as other dramatic changes related to the workplace. As Suze Orman summarizes some of trends in her recent book *Women & Money* (2007, p. 7), "Women make up nearly half of the total workforce in this country. Over the past thirty years, women's income has soared a dramatic 63 percent. Forty-nine percent of all professional-and managerial-level workers are women. Women bring in half or more of the income in the majority of U.S. households—a growing trend that made the cover of

Newsweek and was front page news in many of the nation's newspapers"

Although future cohorts of women undoubtedly will continue to have higher rates of labor force participation, they also will be more likely to enter their retirement years either divorced or in second marriages. Moreover, the age of first marriage continues to rise, and more women are eschewing marriage altogether. Changes in employment and family structure will not alter the risk of poverty that older women may experience. The three legs of financial support for the older population continue to be Social Security, pensions, and assets, with Social Security making up a substantial share of the income of older women.

The changing pension structure in the workplace, as well as looming changes in the benefit structure of Social Security, will continue to negatively affect unmarried women. The privatization of Social Security, which depends on individual initiative, is unlikely to benefit those who may live from paycheck to paycheck. Those who lack the "safety net" of income from a spouse will be at a great disadvantage in this system.

Current events have shown, however, that even this "safety net" is no guarantee of economic security, as it continues to erode for various reasons, including unprecedented unethical and illegal corporate practices. The recent Enron scandal is, of course, an ultimate example of this erosion, as thousands of employees and investors lost all their savings, children's college funds, and pensions when Enron collapsed. Moreover, in most companies, formerly established pensions and medical benefits are changing substantially. According to a recent AARP Bulletin (2007), about 20 percent of the work force is currently in defined benefit plans that guarantee retirement income reduced from 40 percent in 1980. Moreover, plans in place today may change in the future. As the workforce ages, and as the 79 million baby boomers begin to retire, the risks and costs of these plans increase.

In addition, the incomes of older Americans have been deceasing in recent years, as exemplified by their increased use of credit. A study done by the National Consumer Law Center (2006) found that many older consumers are using credit cards as a "plastic safety net" to make essential purchases. The report further documents that some of the key factors that explain the use of credit cards by those 65 and older is a result of their shrinking incomes and higher expenses.

As these trends illustrate, the governmental programs in place to ensure economic security for the elderly population are beginning to disappear. The current political environment and looming radical changes in the Social Security system will result in the economic security of older people evaporating.

Slowly the legs of the "three legged stool" that represent the sources of income for older people are buckling. Regardless of marital status, therefore, both more older women, and a greater percentage of them than ever before, are certain to experience economic insecurity. This negative trend is also likely to affect a greater number and percentage of younger women than ever before.

Already inklings of these adverse changes are being felt, even if subliminally, by women throughout America. As Orman

(2007, p. 8) notes, "Ninety percent of women who participated in a 2006 survey commissioned by Allianz Insurance rated themselves as feeling insecure when it came to their finances. In the same survey, nearly half of the respondents said that the prospect of becoming a bag lady crossed their minds. . . .Nearly 80 percent said they will depend on Social Security in their golden years."

The inevitable changes unfolding in the economic system for women of all marital statuses, especially for unmarried older women, must not be ignored by those with the power to shape social and economic policies.

Failure to act now will guarantee not only a decline in their economic well-being but, much worse, the impoverishment of millions of women in the near future. As the "boomer" generation enters old age, their unprecedented numbers will place impossible demands on our out-dated economic institutions designed to provide support for older Americans.

Changes will need to be implemented on all fronts, including the Social Security system, the pension structure, benefits to retirees in both the private and public sectors, and even the way women view their place in their family that could affect their economic outcomes, among many others. The most urgently needed changes are for older women without spouses, as emphasized in the preceding chapters.

It is certain that Congress eventually will make the changes necessary to address the emerging problems of economic security and well-being discussed and analyzed in this book. The major question is whether we will act to prevent an economic catastrophe before it is too late. As a nation, we have the resources to create just and rational economic institutions, but do we have the will and compassion to "do the right thing"? Only time will tell.

References

Andress, H., Lipsmeier, G., & Lohmann, H. (2001). Income, expenditure and standard of living as poverty indicators—different measures, similar results? *Schmollers Jahrbuch, 121*(2), 165-198.

Arditti, J. A. (1997). Women, divorce, and economic risk. *Family and Conciliation Courts Review, 35*(1), 79-89.

Bardasi, E., Jenkins, S. P., & Rigg, J. A. (2002). Retirement and the income of older people: A British perspective. *Ageing and Society, 22*(2), 131-159.

Barton, L. (1995). Aging and economics: A comparative examination of responses by the United States, Great Britain and Japan. *The International Journal of Sociology and Social Policy, 15*(1-2-3), 120-133.

Barusch, A. S. (2000). Social Security is not for babies: Trends and policies affecting older women in the United States. *Families in Society, 81*(6), 568-575.

Bauman, K. J. (2002). Welfare, work and material hardship in single parent and other households. *Journal of Poverty, 6*(1), 21-40.

Beverly, S. G. (2001). Material hardship in the united states: Evidence from the survey of income and program participation. *Social work research, 25*(3), 143-151.

Bianchi, S. (1995). The changing demographic and socioeconomic characteristics of single parent families. (Single parent families: Diversity, myths, and realities, part 1). *Marriage and Family Review 20*(1-2): 71-98).

Bianchi, S. M., Casper, L. M., & Peltola, P. K. (1999). A cross-national look at married women's earnings dependency. *Gender Issues, 17*(3), 3-33.

Biddlecom, A. E., & Kramarow, E. A. (1998). Household headship among married women: The roles of economic power, education, and convention. *Journal of Family and Economic Issues, 19*(4), 367-382.

Borooah, V. K., McGregor, P. P., & McKee, P. M. (1995). Working wives and income inequality in the UK. *Regional Studies, 29*(5), 477-487.

Bound, J., Duncan, G. J., Laren, D. S., & Olenick, L. (1991). Poverty dynamics in widowhood. *Journal of Gerontology: Social Sciences, 46,* S115-S1124.

Brandon, P. D. (1999). Income-pooling arrangements, economic constraints, and married mothers' child care choices. *Journal of Family Issues, 20*(3), 350-370.

Brandon, P. D., & Fisher, G. A. (2001). The dissolution of joint living arrangements among single parents and children: Does welfare make a difference? *Social Science Quarterly, 82*(1), 1-19.

Brines, J., & Joyner, K. (1999). The ties that bind: Principles of cohesion in cohabitation and marriage. *American Sociological Review, 64*(3), 333-355.

Buckhauser, R. V., Butrica, B. A., & Wasylenko, M. J. (1995). Mobility patterns of older homeowners: Are older homeowners trapped in distressed neighborhoods? *Research on Aging, 17*(4), 363-384.

Burkhauser, R., Butler, J., Holden, K. (1991) How the death of a spouse affects the economic well-being after retirement: A hazard model approach. *Social Science Quarterly, 72* (3), 504-520.

Burkhauser, R. & Duncan, G. (1989). Economic risks of gender roles: Income loss and life events over the life course. *Social Science Quarterly, 70,* 3-23.

Butrica, B. A. & Iams, H. M. (2003). The impact of minority group status on the projected retirement income of divorced women in the baby boom cohort. *Journal of women & Aging, 15*(2-3), 67-88.

Byles, J. E., Feldman, S., & Mishra, G. (1999). For richer, for poorer, in sickness and in health: Older widowed women's health, relationships and financial security. *Women and Health, 29*(1), 15-30.

Cain, B. S. (1988). Divorce among elderly women: A growing social phenomenon. *The Journal of Contemporary Social Work*. November.

Cancian, M., & Reed, D. (1999). The impact of wives' earnings on income inequality: Issues and estimates. *Demography, 36*(2), 173-184.

Cheal, D. (2004). Intergenerational transfers. *Journal of Marriage and the Family, 45*(4), 805-813.

Chen, C. (2001). Aging and life satisfaction. *Social Indicators Research, 54*(1), 57-79.

Cherlin, A. J. (1998). Marriage and marital dissolution among black Americans. (Special issue: Comparative perspectives on black family life, vol. 1). *Journal of Comparative Family Studies, 29*(1), 147-159.

_____. (1992). M*arriage, divorce, remarriage*. Harvard College Press.

Chevan, A. (1995). Holding on and letting go: Residential mobility during widowhood. *Research on aging, 17*(3), 278-302.

Childers, C. D. (1999). Elderly female-headed households in the disaster loan process. *International Journal of Mass Emergencies and Disasters, 17*(1), 99-110.

Choi, N. (1992). Correlates of the economic status of widowed and divorced elderly women. *Journal of Family Issues, 13*(1), 38-54.

_____. (1997). Racial differences in retirement income: The roles of public and private income sources. *Journal of Aging and Social Policy, 9*(3), 21-43.

Choudury, S. & Leonesio, M. (1997). Life cycle aspects of poverty among older women. *Social Security Bulletin, 60*(2), 17-37.

_____. (1998). Poverty among Older Women. *Family Economics and Nutritional Review, 11*(3), 71-73.

Clydesdale, T. T. (1997). Family behaviors among early U.S. baby boomers: Exploring the effects of religion and income change, 1965-1982. *Social Forces, 76*(2), 605-635.

Couto, R. A. (2003). It takes a pillage: Women, work, and welfare. *Race, Gender & Class, 10*(1), 60-78.

Crystal, S. & Shea, D. (1990). Cumulative advantage, cumulative disadvantage, and inequality among elderly people. *The Gerontologist, 30*(4), 437-443.

Curtis, L., & Phipps, S. (2004). Social transfers and the health status of mothers in Norway and Canada. *Social Science & Medicine, 58*(12), 2499-2507.

Danigelis, N. L., & McIntosh, B. R. (2001). Gender's effect on the relationships linking older Americans' resources and financial satisfaction. *Research on aging, 23*(4), 410-428.

Davies, S. & Denton, M. (2002). The economic well-being of older women who become divorced or separated in mid- or later life. *Canadian Journal on Aging/La Revue Canadienne du Vieillissement, 21*(4), 477-493.

Davies, H., Joshi, H., & Peronaci, R. (2000). Forgone income and motherhood: What do recent British data tell us? *Population Studies, 54*(3), 293-305.

Davis, N. J., & Robinson, R. V. (1998). Do wives matter? Class identities of wives and husbands in the united states, 1974-1994. *Social Forces, 76*(3), 1063-1086.

de Barros, P. & de Mendonca, P. (1992). The evolution of well-being and inequality in Brazil since 1960. *Econpapers, 49*(2), 18-27.

Del Boca, D., Locatelli, M., & Pasqua, S. (2000). Employment decisions of married women: Evidence and explanations. *Labour, 14*(1), 35-52.

DeShane, M. R. & Brown-Wilson, K. (1981). Divorce in late life: A call for research. *Journal of Divorce, 4*(4), 81-91.

DeViney, S. (1995). Life course, private pension and financial well-being. *American Behavioral Scientist, 39*(2), 172-186.

DeViney, S., & Solomon, J. C. (1995). Gender differences in retirement income: A comparison of theoretical explanations. *Journal of women & aging, 7*(4), 83-100.

Dinkins, J. M. (1995). Per capita income and expenditures of baby-boomer households. *Family Economics and Nutrition Review, 8*(3), 27-39.

Dixon, C. S., & Rettig, K. D. (1994). An examination of income adequacy for single women two years after divorce. *Journal of Divorce and Remarriage, 22*, 55-71.

Dolan, M. A., & Hoffman, C. D. (1998). Determinants of divorce among women: A reexamination of critical influences. *Journal of Divorce and Remarriage, 28*(3-4), 97-106.

Duncan, G. J. & Hoffman, S. D. (1985). *Economic consequences of marital instability in horizontal equity, uncertainty, and economic well-being.* Chicago: University of Chicago Press.

Easterlin, R. A. (1996). Economic and social implications of demographic patterns. In *Handbook of aging and the social sciences*. R. H. Binstock & Linda K. George (eds). New York: Academy Press.

Edin, K. (2000). Few good men: Why poor women don't remarry. *The American Prospect, 28,* 26-31.

Edwards, M. E. (2001). Home ownership, affordability, and mothers' changing work and family roles. *Social Science Quarterly, 82*(2), 369-383.

Elder, G. H., Jr. & O'Rand, A. (1994). Adult lives in a changing society. In *Sociological perspectives in social psychology*. J. S. Hook & G. Fine (eds.) Boston: Allyn & Bacon.

Elder, G. H., Jr. (1995). The life course paradigm: social change and individual development. In E*xamining lives in context: Perspectives on the ecology of human development.* Phyllis Moen, Glen Elder, Jr., & Kurt Luscher (eds.).Washington, D.C.: American Psychological Association.

Elder, G. H., Jr. (1985). *Life course dynamics.* Ithica, NY: Cornell University Press.

Elman, C. (1996). Old age, economic activity, and living arrangements in the early-twentieth-century united states. *Social Science History, 20*(3), 439-468.

Esping-Anderson, G. (1990). *The three worlds of welfare capitalism.* NJ: Princeton University Press.

Estes, C., Linkins, K., & Binney, E. (1996). The political economy of aging. In *Handbook of aging and the social sciences* (4th edition). R. H. Binstock & L. K. George (Eds.). San Diego: Academic Press.

Evandrou, M., & Glaser, K. (2004). Family, work and quality of life: Changing economic and social roles through the life-course. *Ageing & Society, 24*(5), 771-791.

_____. (1985). Perspectives on the life course. In *Life course dynamics:Trajectories and transitions, 1968-1980.* Cornell University Press.

Farkas, J. I. & O'Rand, A. (1998). The pension mix for women in middle and late life: The changing employment relationship. *Social Forces, 76*(3), 1007-1033.

Fethke, C.C. (1984). An economic model of asset division in the dissolution of marriage. *American Economic Review, 74,* 265-270.

_____. (1989). Life-cycle models of saving and the effect of the timing of divorce on retirement economic well-being. *Journal of Gerontology: Social Sciences, 44,* S121-128.

Fitzpatrick, T. R., & Vinick, B. (2003). The impact of husbands' retirement on wives' marital quality. *Journal of Family Social Work, 7*(1), 83-100.

Flavin, M.A. 1981. The adjustment of consumption to changing expectations about future income. *Journal of Political Economy, 89,* 974-1009

Garfinkle, I. & McLanahan, S. (1986). *Single mothers and their children: A new American dilemma.* Washington, D.C.: Urban Institute.

Garfinkle, I., McLanahan, S. & Watson, D. (1989). Divorce, female headship, and child support. In W*omen's life cycle and economic insecurity: Problems and proposals.* Martha N. Ozawa (ed.). New York: Greenwood Press.

George, L. K. (1993). Sociological perspectives on life transitions. *Annual Review of Sociology. 19,* 353-373.

Gerdtham, U. & Johannesson, M. (2001). The relationship between happiness, health, and socio-economic factors: Results based on swedish microdata. *Journal of Socio-economics, 30*(6), 553-557.

Glick, P. & Lin, S. (1986). Remarriage after divorce. *Sociological perspectives, 30*(2), 162- 180.

Goetting, M. A., Raiser, M. V., Martin, P., Poon, L. W., & Johnson, M. A. (1995). Older women's financial resources and perception of financial adequacy. *Journal of Women & Aging, 7*(4), 67-81.

Goldin, C. (1990). *Understanding the gender gap.* New York: Oxford University Press.

Goldscheider, F. & Goldsheider, C. (2004). The intergenerational flow of income: Family structure and the status of black Americans. *Journal of Marriage and the Family, 53* (2), 499-508.

Gonzalez, L. (2004). Single mothers and work. *Socio-Economic Review, 2*(2), 285-313.

Goodfellow, G. & Scheiber, S. (1993). The role of tax expenditure in the provision of retirement income security. In *Pensions in a changing economy.* Richard V. Burkhauser and Dallas L. Salisbury (Eds.). Washington, D.C.: National Academy on Aging and Employee Benefit Research Institute.

Gorman, E. H. (1999). Bringing home the bacon: Marital allocation of income-earning responsibility, job shifts, and men's wages. *Journal of Marriage and the Family, 61*(1), 110-122.

Gornick, J. C. (2004). Women's economic outcomes, gender inequality and public policy: Findings from the luxembourg income study. *Socio-Economic Review, 2*(2), 213-238.

Gough, O. (2001). The impact of the gender pay gap on post-retirement earnings. *Critical Social Policy, 21*(68), 311-334.

Gray, T. (2005). Pension roulette: Millions of Americans are losing benefits. How Secure is your future? *AARP Bulletin.* http://www.aarp.org/bulletine/yourmoney/pension_rulette.html.

Gunnlaugsson, G. A., & Gardarsdottir, O. (1996). Transition into widowhood: A life-course perspective on the household position of icelandic widows at the beginning of the twentieth century. *Continuity and Change, 11*(3), 435-458.

Gyamfi, P., Brooks-Gunn, J. & Jackson, A. P. (2001) Associations between employment and parental stress in low-income single black households. *Women and Health,* 32(1), 119-136.

Han, S. & Moen, P. (1999). Work and family over time: A life course approach. *The Annals of the American Academy of Political and Social Science, 562,* 98-110.

Hanson, S. L. (1983). A family life-cycle approach to the socioeconomic attainment of working women. *Journal of Marriage and Family, 42*(2), 323-338.

Hanson, T. L., McLanahan, S. S., & Thompson, E. (1998). Windows on divorce: Before and after. *Social Science Research, 27*(3), 329-349.

Hao, L. (1996). Family structure, private transfers, and the economic well-being of families with children. *Social Forces, 75,* 269-292.

Hardy, M., & Hazelrigg, L. (1993). The gender of poverty in an aging population. *Research on Aging, 15,* 243-278.

Harrington-Meyer, M. (1990). Family status and poverty among older women: The gendered distribution of retirement income in the united states. *Social Problems, 37*(4), 551-563.

_____. (1996). Making claims as workers or wives: The distribution of Social Security benefits. *American Sociological Review, 61,* 449-465.

Harrington-Myer, M., Street, D., & Quadagno, J. (1994). The impact of family status on income security and health care in old age: A comparison of western nations. *International journal of sociology and social policy, 14* (1-2), 53-83.

Hatch, L. (1990). Effects of work and family on women's later-life resources. *Research on Aging, 12,* 311-338.

Hazelrigg, L., & Hardy, M. (1997). Perceived income adequacy among older adults: Issues of conceptualization and measurement, with an analysis of data. *Research on Aging, 19*(1), 69-107.

He, Wan, Sengupta M., Velkoff, V., & DeBurros, K. (2006). 65+ in the United States: 2005. *Current Population Reports Special Studies.* U.S. Census Bureau. (http: www.census.gov/)

Heckert, D. A., Nowak, T. C., & Snyder, K. A. (1998). The impact of husbands' and wives' relative earnings on marital disruption. *Journal of Marriage and the Family, 60*(3), 690-703.

Heimdal, K. R., & Houseknecht, S. K. (2003). Cohabiting and married couples' income organization: Approaches in Sweden and the United States. *Journal of Marriage and Family, 65*(3), 525-538.

Henretta, J. & Campbell, R. T. (1976). Status attainment and status maintenance: A study of stratification in old age. *American Sociological Review, 76*(4), 981-992.

Hirschl, T. A., Altobelli, J., & Rank, M. R. (2003). Does marriage increase the odds of affluence? Exploring the life course probabilities. *Journal of Marriage and Family, 65*(4), 927-938.

Hoffman, S. (1977). Marital instability and the economic status of women. D*emography, 14*(1), 67-77.

Hogan, R., Perrucci, C., & Behringer, A. (2005). Enduring inequality: Gender and employment income in late career. *Sociological Spectrum, 25*(1), 53-77.

Hogan, R., & Perrucci, C. (1998). Producing and reproducing class and status differences: Racial and gender gaps in U.S. employment and retirement income. *Social Problems, 45*(4), 528-549.

Holden, K., Burkhauser, R. & Feaster, D. J. (1988). The timing of falls into poverty after retirement and widowhood. *Demography, 25*(3), 405-414.

Holden, K., Burkhauser, R. & Myers, D. (1986). Marital disruption and poverty: The role of survey procedures in artifically creating poverty. *Demography, 23*(4), 621-631.

Holden, K. & Kuo, D. (1996). Complex marital histories and economic well- being: The continuing legacy of divorce and widowhood. *The Gerontologist, 36*(3), 383-391.

Holden, K. & Myers, D. A. (1986). Income transitions at older stages of life: The dynamics of poverty. *The Gerontologist, 26*(3), 292-297.

Holden, K. & Smock, P. (1991). The economic costs of marital disruption: Why do women bear a disproportionate cost? *Annual Review of Sociology, 17*(1), 51-78.

Hungerford, T. L. (2001). The economic consequences of widowhood on elderly women in the United States and Germany. *Gerontologist, 41*(1), 103-110.

Hurd, M. D. & Wise, D. A. (1989). The wealth and poverty of widows: Assets before and after the husband's death. In *Economics of Aging,* David Wise (ed.). Chicago and London.: The University of Chicago Press.

Hyde, M., Ferrie, J., Higgs, P., Mein, G., & Nazroo, J. (2004). The effects of pre-retirement factors and retirement route on circumstances in retirement: Findings from the whitehall II study. *Ageing & Society, 24*(2), 279-296.

Jalovaara, M. (2001). Socio-economic status and divorce in first marriages in Finland 1991-93. *Population Studies, 55*(2), 119-133.

Janzen, B. L., & Muhajarine, N. (2003). Social role occupancy, gender, income adequacy, life stage and health: A longitudinal study of employed Canadian men and women. *Social Science & Medicine, 57*(8), 1491-1503.

Jones, S. (1999). Singlehood for security: Towards a review of the relative economic status of women and children in woman-led households. *Society in Transition, 30*(1), 13-27.

Kart, C. S. (1997).

Juster, F. & Suzman, R. (1995). An overview of the health and retirement study. *Journal of Human Resources, 30*(5), S7-S56.

Kart, C. S. (1997). *The realities of aging: An introduction to gerontology.* Boston: Allyn and Bacon

Keister, L. A., & Deeb-Sossa, N. (2001). Are baby boomers richer than their parents? Intergenerational patterns of wealth ownership in the united states. Journal of *Marriage and the Family, 63*(2), 569-579.

Kenney, C. (2004). Cohabiting couple, filing jointly? Resource pooling and U.S. poverty policies. *Family Relations, 53*(2), 237-247.

Kivett, V. & Schwenk, F. (1994). The consumer expenditures of elderly women: Racial, marital, and rural-urban impacts. *Journal of Family and Economic Issues, 15*(3), 261-277.

Knotter, A. (2004). Poverty and the family-income cycle: Casual laborers in Amsterdam in the first half of the 20th century. The *History of the Family, 9*(2), 221-237.

Kotlikoff, L. J. & Morris, J. N. (1989). How much care do the aged receive from their adult children? A bimodal picture of contact and assistance. In *The Economics of Aging.* David A. Wise (ed.). Chicago: University at Chicago Press.

Krueger, P. M., Rogers, R. G., Hummer, R. A., LeClere, F. B., & Bond Huie, S. A. (2003). Socioeconomic status and age: The effect of income sources and portfolios on U.S. adult mortality. *Sociological Forum, 18*(3), 465-482.

Laditka, J. N., & Laditka, S. B. (2000). Aging children and their older parents: The coming generation of caregiving. *Journal of Women & Aging, 12*(1-2), 189-204.

Lillard, L. A., & Waite, L. J. (1995). 'Til death do us part: Marital disruption and mortality. *American Journal of Sociology, 100*(5), 1131-1156.

_____. (1993). A joint model of marital childbearing and marital disruption. *Demography 30*(4), 653-662.

Lino, M. (1996). Expenditures on children by families, 1995 Annual Report, U.S. Department of Agriculture, Center for Nutrition Policy and Promotion, Washington D.C.

Loew, R. M. (1995). Determinants of divorced older women's labor supply. *Research on Aging, 17*(4), 385-411.

London, R. A. (2000). The dynamics of single mothers' living arrangements. *Population Research and Policy Review, 19*(1), 73-96.

Loonin, D., Devanthery J., & Tripoli, S. (2006). *The Life and Debt Cycle Part One: The Implications of Rising Credit Card Debt among Older Consumers.* National Consumer Law Center. http://www.consumerlaw.org.

Marks, N. F., & Choi, H. (2002). Social inequalities, psychological well-being, and health: Longitudinal evidence from a U.S. national study. *Research in the Sociology of Health Care, 20,* 79-106.

Marshall, K. (2000). Incomes of younger retired women: The past 30 years. *Perspectives on Labour and Income, 12*(4), 9-17.

Mathieson, K. M., Kronenfeld, J. J., & Keith, V. M. (2002). Maintaining functional independence in elderly adults: The roles of health status and financial resources in predicting home modifications and use of mobility equipment. *Gerontologist, 42*(1), 24-31.

Maudlin, T. A. (1990). Women who remain above the poverty level in divorce: Implications for family policy. *Family Relations, 39,* 141-146.

Maume, D. J., Jr. (2004). Wage discrimination over the life course: A comparison of explanations. *Social problems, 51*(4), 505-527.

McGarry, K., & Schoeni, R. F. (2000). Social security, economic growth, and the rise in elderly widows' independence in the twentieth century. *Demography, 37*(2), 221-236.

McLaughlin, D. K. (1998). Rural women's economic realities. *Journal of Women & Aging, 10*(4), 41-65.

Miller, N. B., Smerglia, V. L., Gaudet, D. S., & Kitson, G. C. (1998). Stressful life events, social support, and the distress of widowed and divorced women: A counteractive model. *Journal of Family Issues, 19*(2), 181-203.

Mirowsky, J., & Ross, C. E. (1999). Economic hardship across the life course. *American Sociological Review, 64*(4), 548-569.

Moen, P. (1996). Gender, age, and the life course. In *Handbook of aging and the social sciences*. Robert H. Binstock and Linda K. George (eds.). New York: Academy Press.

_____. (1985). Continuities and discontinuities in women's labor force activity. In *Life Course Dynamic: Trajectories and Transitions, 1968-1980.* Glen H. Elder, Jr. (ed.). Ithaca and London: Cornell University Press.

Montalto, C. P., & Gerner, J. L. (1998). The effect of expected changes in marital status on labor supply decisions of women and men. *Journal of Divorce and Remarriage, 28*(3-4), 25-51.

Morgan, L. A. (2000). The continuing gender gap in later life economic security. *Journal of Aging & Social Policy, 11*(2-3), 157-165.

_____. (1991). *After marriage ends: Economic consequences for midlife women.* CA: Sage Publications.

_____. (1989). Economic well-being following marital termination: A comparison of widowed and divorced women. *Journal of Family Issues, 10,* 86-101.

_____. (1981). Economic change at mid-life widowhood: A longitudinal analysis. *Journal of Marriage and the Family,* 899-907.

Myles, J. (2000). The maturation of Canada's retirement income system: Income levels, income inequality and low income among older persons. Canadian *Journal on Aging/La Revue Canadienne du Vieillissement, 19*(3), 287-316.

Myles, J., & Street, D. (1995). Should the economic life course be redesigned? Old age security in a time of transition. *Canadian Journal on Aging/La Revue Canadienne du Vieillissement, 14*(2), 335-359.

Norton, A. J. & Moorman, J. E. (1987). Current trends in marriage and divorce among american women. *Journal of Marriage and Family, 49*(1), 3-14.

O'Bryant, S. L. & Morgan, L. A. (1989). Financial experience and well-being among mature widowed women. *The Gerontologist, 29*(2), 245-251.

Ofstedal, M. B., Reidy, E., & Knodel, J. (2004). Gender differences in economic support and well-being of older Asians. *Journal of Cross-Cultural Gerontology, 19*(3), 165-201.

O'Grady-LeShane, R. (1990). Older women and poverty. *Social Work, 35* (5), 422-434.

O'Rand, A. (1996). The Precious and the precocious: Understanding cumulative disadvantage and cumulative advantage over the life course. *The Gerontologist, 36,* 230-238.

O'Rand, A. & Henretta, J. C. (1982). Delayed career entry, industrial pension structure, and early retirement in a cohort of unmarried women. *American Sociological Review, 47,* 365-373.

_____. (1999). *Age and inequality: Diverse pathways through later life.* Colorado: Westview Press.

O'Rand, A. & Landerman, R. (1984). Women's and men's retirement Income status: Early family role effects. *Research on Aging, 6,* 25-44.

Orman, S. (2007). *Women & money: Owning the power to control your destiny.* New York: Spiegel and Grau.

Oropesa, R. S., Landale, N. S., & Kenkre, T. (2003). Income allocation in marital and cohabiting unions: The case of mainland Puerto Ricans. *Journal of Marriage and Family, 65*(4), 910-926.

Oygard, L. (2004). Divorce support groups: What is the role of the participants' personal capital regarding adjustment to divorce? *Journal of Divorce and Remarriage, 40*(3-4), 103-119.

Ozawa, M. N. (1995). The economic status of vulnerable older women. *Social Work, 40*(3), 323-331.

Ozawa, M. N., & Hong, B. (2001). Economic class and redistribution of income through spousal benefits under Social Security. *Journal* of Poverty, 5(3), 1-16.

Ozawa, M. N., & Kim, H. (2001). Money's worth in Social Security benefits: Black-white differences. *Social Work Research, 25*(1), 5-14.

Ozawa, M. N., & Tseng, H. (2000). Differences in net worth between elderly black people and elderly white people. *Social Work Research, 24*(2), 96-108.

Ozawa, M. N., & Yoon, H. (2002). Social Security and SSI as safety nets for the elderly poor. *Journal of Aging & Social Policy, 14*(2), 1-25.

Peters, A., & Liefbroer, A. C. (1997). Beyond marital status: Partner history and well-being in old age. *Journal of Marriage and the Family, 59*(3), 687-699.

Peterson, R. R. (1989). *Women, work, and divorce.* Albany, NY: State University of New York Press.

Pezzin, L. & Steinberg-Schone, B. (1999). Parental marital disruption and intergenerational transfers: An analysis of lone elderly parents and their children. *Demography, 36*(3), 287-297.

Pienta, A., Burr, J., & Mutchler, N. (1994). Women's labor force participationm in later life: The effects of early work and family experiences. Journal of Gerontology: *Social Sciences, 49,* S231-S239.

Pollock, G. E., & Stroup, A. L. (1996). Economic consequences of marital dissolution for blacks. *Journal of Divorce and Remarriage, 26*(1-2), 49-67.

Prus, S. (2000). Income inequality as a Canadian cohort ages—an analysis of the later life course. *Research on Aging, 22,* 211-237.

Rabusic, L. (2004). Why are they all so eager to retire? *Sociologicky Casopis, 40*(3), 319-342.

Robert, S. A., & Li, L. W. (2001). Age variation in the relationship between community socioeconomic status and adult health. *Research on Aging, 23*(2), 233-258.

Robison, L. J., & Siles, M. E. (1999). Social capital and household income distributions in the United States: 1980-1990. *Journal of Socio-Economics, 28*(1), 43-93.

Rodgers, S. J. (1999). Wives' income and marital quality: Are there reciprocal effects? *Journal of Marriage and the Family, 61*(1), 123-132.

Rogers, S. J., & DeBoer, D. D. (2001). Changes in wives' income: Effects on marital happiness, psychological well-being, and the risk of divorce. *Journal of Marriage and the Family, 63*(2), 458-472.

Roos, P. A. (1983). Marriage and women's occupational attainment in cross-cultural perspective. *American Sociological Review, 48,* 852-64.

Rubin, R. M., & Nieswiadomy, M. L. (1995). Economic adjustments of households on entry into retirement. *Journal of Applied Gerontology, 14*(4), 467-482.

Ruble, M., Patton, R. & Nelson, D. (2000). Patton-Nelson personal consumption tables: 1997-98 update. *Journal of Forensic Economics, 13*(3), 303-307.

Sadar, N. C., & Iskra, A. B. (1996). Material quality of life in various life cycles. *Druzboslovne Razprave, 12*(22-23), 72-83.

Schoen, R., Urton, W., Woodrow, K., & Baj, J. (1985). Marriage and Divorce in twentieth–century American cohorts. *Demography, 22,* 101-114.

Schuchardt, J. & Guadagno, M. (1991). A comparison of lower middle-income two-parent and single-mother families. *Home Economics Review, 4*(2), 9-17

Shaw, K. (1992). The life-cycle labor supply of married women and its implications for household income inequality. *Economic Inquiry, 30*(4), 659-72

Silver, H., & Miller, S. M. (2003). Social exclusion. *Indicators*, 2(2), 5-21.

Singh, S., & Lindsay, J. (1996). Money in heterosexual relationships. The Australian and New Zealand Journal of Sociology, 32(3), 57-69.

Smeeding, T. M. (2004). Twenty years of research on income inequality, poverty, and redistribution in the developed world: Introduction and overview. Socio-Economic Review, 2(2), 149-163.

Smith, K. R., & Zick, C. D. (1996). Risk of mortality following widowhood: Age and sex differences by mode of death. Social biology, 43(1-2), 59-71.

_____. (1986). The incidence of poverty among the recent widowed: Mediating factors in the life course. Journal of Marriage and Family, 48, 619-630.

Smock, P. J., Manning, W. D., & Gupta, S. (1999). The effect of marriage and divorce on women's economic well-being. American Sociological Review, 64, 794-812.

Sorensen, A. & McLanahan, S. (1987). Married women's economic dependency. *American Journal of Sociology, 93*, 659-687.

South, S. J. & Spitze, G. (1986). Determinants of divorce over the marital life course. American Sociological Review, 51, 583-590.

Spratlin, J. & Holden, K. C. (2000). Women and economic security in retirement: Implications for Social Security reform. Journal of Family and Economic Issues, 21(1), 37-63.

Stirling, K. J. (1989). Women who remain divorced: The long-term economic consequences. *Social Science Quarterly, 70*, 549-561.

Stoller, M. A., & Stoller, E. P. (2003). Perceived income adequacy among elderly retirees. *The Journal of Applied Gerontology, 22*(2), 230-251.

Street, D. & Wilmoth, J. (2001). Social insecurity? Women and pensions in the U.S. In Ginn et al. (eds), Women, work, and pensions: International issues and prospects. Philadelphia: Open University Press.

Stroup, A. L. & Pollock, G. E. (1999). Economic well-being among elderly white divorced. *Journal of Divorce and Remarriage, 31,* 53-68.

Szinovacz, M. E., & DeViney, S. (2000). Marital characteristics and retirement decisions. *Research on Aging, 22*(5), 470-498.

Tabbarah, M., Silverstein, M., & Seeman, T. (2000). A health and demographic profile of noninstitutionalized older americans residing in environments with home modifications. *Journal of Aging and Health, 12*(2), 204-228.

Teachman, J. D., Tedrow, L. M., & Crowder, K. D. (2000). The changing demography of America's families. *Journal of Marriage and the Family, 62*(4), 1234-1246.

Tzeng, J. M., & Mare, R. D. (1995). Labor market and socioeconomic effects on marital stability. *Social Science Research, 24*(4), 329-351.

Uhlenberg, P., Cooney, T., & Boyd, R. (1990). Divorce for women after midlife. *Journal of Gerontology: Social Sciences, 45*(1), S3-11.

Uhlenberg, P. & Myers, M. (1981). Divorce and the elderly. *The Gerontologist, 21*, 276-282.

U.S. Department of Labor: Women's Bureau. 2007. *Older women workers, Ages 55 and over.* http: www.dol.gov/wb/

_____. *Women in the Labor Force in 2006.* http: www.dol.gov/wb/

Van Berkel, M., & De Graaf, N. D. (1998). Married women's economic dependency in the Netherlands, 1979-1991. *The British Journal of Sociology, 49*(1), 97-117.

Vartanian, T. P., & McNamara, J. M. (2002). Older women in poverty: The impact of midlife factors. *Journal of Marriage and the Family, 64*(2), 532-548.

Waite, L. J. (1999). The negative effects of cohabitation. *The Responsive Community, 10*(1), 31-38.

Waite, L. J. (1996). Social science finds: "Marriage matters." *The Responsive Community, 6*(3), 26-35.

Wakita, S., Fitzsimmons, V. S., & Liao, T. F. (2000). Wealth: Determinants of savings net worth and housing net worth of pre-retired households. *Journal of Family and Economic Issues, 21*(4), 387-418.

Wang, H., & Amato, P. R. (2000). Predictors of divorce adjustment: Stressors, resources, and definitions. *Journal of Marriage and the Family, 62*(3), 655-668.

Weitzman, L. (1985). *The divorce revolution: The unexpected social and economic consequences for women and children in America.* NY: The Free Press.

Williams, J. H., Auslander, W. F., Houston, C. A., Krebill, H., & Haire-Joshu, D. (2000). African-American family structure: Are there differences in social, psychological, and economic well-being? *Journal of Family Issues, 21*(7), 838-857.

Williamson, J. B. & McNamara, T. K. (2003). Interrupted trajectories and labor force participation: The effect of unplanned changes in marital and disability status. *Research on Aging, 25*(2), 87-121.

Williamson, J. B., & Rix, S. E. (2000). Social Security reform: Implications for women. *Journal of Aging & Social Policy, 11*(4), 41-68.

Willson, A. E. (2003). Race and women's income trajectories: Employment, marriage and income security over the life course. *Social Problems, 50,* 87-119.

Willson, A. E., & Hardy, M. A. (2002). Racial disparities in income security for a cohort of aging American women. *Social Forces, 80*(4), 1283-1306.

Wilmoth, J. & Koso, G. (2002). Does marital status matter? Marital status and wealth outcomes among preretirement adults. *Journal of Marriage and Family, 64,* 254-268.

Zhan, M., & Pandey, S. (2004). Economic well-being of single mothers: Work first or postsecondary education? *Journal of Sociology and Social Welfare, 31*(3), 87-112.

Zhan, M., & Sherraden, M. (2003). Assets, expectations, and children's educational achievement in female-headed households. *Social Service Review, 77*(2), 191-211.

Zick, C. D., Fan, J. X., & Chang, K. (2004). Impending widowhood and health care spending. *Social Science Research, 33*(3), 538-555.

Zick, C. D. & Smith, K. R. (1988). Recent widowhood, remarriage, and changes in economic well-being. *Journal of Marriage and Family, 50*, 233-244.

Zsembik, B. A., Drevenstedt, G. L., & McLane, C. P. (1997). Economic well-being among older Latinos. *The International Journal of Sociology and Social Policy, 17*(9-10), 34-56.

Appendix 1: The Rand Heath & Retirement Study

The Health and Retirement Study is a nationally representative survey of 7,706 households with at least one person age 51-61 (Juster & Suzman, 1995). Funded by the National Institute on Aging (NIA) with supplemental support from the Social Security Administration, the Assistant Secretary for Planning and Evaluation (ASPE) in the U.S. Department of Health and Human services (DHHS), and the Pension and Welfare Benefit Office, it is conducted by the Institute for Social Research (ISR), the University of Michigan, Ann Arbor. It was joined in 1993 by a companion study, Assets and Health Dynamics of the Oldest Old (AHEAD), consisting of persons born before 1924 who were aged 70 and over in 1993.

The HRS was originally designed to follow age-eligible individuals and their spouses as they made the transition from active worker into retirement. The AHEAD study was designed to examine the dynamic interactions between health, family, and economic variables in the post-retirement period at the end of life.

Supported by funding from the National Institute of Aging (NIA) and the Social Security Administration (SSA), the Rand HRS is a "user-friendly" version of the HRS. It contains cleaned and processed variables with consistent naming conventions. The Rand HRS is the result of three distinct data developments. With funding from the NIA, "flat-files" were created of each survey wave. In these files, the unit of analysis is an individual respondent. The files contain all unrestricted variables from the HRS. With funding from the SSA, a longitudinal file was created, and in collaboration with staff from the HRS at the University of Michigan, the file was made publicly available on the HRS web site (http://hrsonline.isr.umich.edu).

Data were collected for the HRS in 1992, 1994, and 1996. AHEAD data were collected in 1993 and 1995, with Wave 1 completed in 1994 and Wave 2 completed in 1996. In 1998, the HRS and AHEAD studies were merged into a single data collection endeavor. The revised study (1998 HRS) included Wave 4 of the HRS and Wave 3 of the AHEAD. Baseline information was added for two new sub-samples: Children of the Depression, the CODA cohort, consisting of persons born between the years 1924 and 1930; and the War Baby (WB) cohort, composed of individuals born between 1942 and 1947.

The 1998 HRS is a panel study, representing all persons over 50 years of age in the United States. This merger included both the original HRS and AHEAD cohort linkages, which permitted longitudinal analysis over all interview years. In 1998 and every two years thereafter, the original HRS sample, the AHEAD sample, and the two new sub-samples—War Babies (WB) and Children of the Depression (CODA)—were interviewed.

The HRS is intended to provide data to those researchers, policy analysts, and program planners who are interested in the retirement behavior, health, savings, and economic well-being of individuals in their later years of life. The objectives of the study are to explain the behavior prior to and the consequences of retirement. The relationship between health, income, and wealth over time is also examined in this study, as well as life cycle patterns of wealth accumulation and consumption. In sum, the main objective of the study is to examine how economic, family, and program resources affect key outcomes for individuals, which include retirement, health declines, and institutionalization.

Questionnaire topics include the following: health, cognitive conditions and status, retirement plans, family structure and transfers, employment status and job history, job demands and requirements, disability, demographic background, housing, income and net worth, health insurance, and pension plans. In addition, there are linkages to pension information from the Employer Pension Study of 1993 and 1999, Medicare claims and summary files, cause of death from the NCHS National Death Index, and earnings, benefits, wage, self-employment income, and SSI data derived form Social Security administrative files. Access is restricted, however, to some of these data.

The HRS core sample is a nationally representative, multi-stage probability sample of non-institutionalized adults. However, individuals are followed if they move from the household into institutions. The core sample is supplemented by a 1.86:1 oversample of African Americans; a 1.72:1 oversample of Hispanics; and a 2:1 oversample of Floridians. Inclusion of the oldest old households with extremely frail respondents was a consideration; therefore a second sampling frame—the Health Care Financing Administration (HCFA) Enrollment base—also was employed.

The sample is selected under a multi-stage probability sample design, and includes four distinct selection stages consisting of households. The units of analysis are household financial units that must include at least one age-eligible member from the designated birth cohorts, and consists of a single unmarried age-eligible person; a married couple in which both persons are age-eligible; or a married couple in which one spouse is age-eligible. If a sample housing unit contains more than one unrelated age-eligible person, then one of these persons is randomly selected as the financial respondent to be observed. If an age-eligible spouse is in the household, then that spouse is automatically selected to be in the sample, even though he or she is not age-eligible.

As discussed earlier, the 1998 HRS is a merged survey consisting of both Wave 4 of the HRS and Wave 3 of the AHEAD study. Therefore, the sample design of those surveys will be outlined. The target population for Wave 4 of the HRS, interviewed in the Spring of 1992, includes all adults in the contiguous United States born during the years 1931-1941 who reside in households. The target population of the AHEAD survey consists of those individuals born in 1923 or earlier. These individuals were interviewed in 1993-94, 1995-96, 1998, and every two years thereafter. The War Baby cohort, added in 1998, consists of those individuals born between 1942 and 1947. The sample design employed was the same as that of the original HRS. The sub-sample was interviewed in 1998 and every two years thereafter. The sample of the Children of the Depression (CODA) cohort—the 1924-1930 birth cohort—was drawn from a stratified sample from a list frame of Medicare enrollees from the Health Care Financing Administration (HCFA) Enrollment. It consists of people born before 1924. They also were interviewed every two years thereafter. The initial sample consisted of over 22,000 persons.

In 2000, the sample interviewed consisted of the four sub-samples described above. The sample interviewed for the 2002 collection period was comprised of slightly different sub-samples. The first sub-sample, the HRS sample, consists of people who were residents of households in the United States (as outlined above) and their spouses or partners at the time of the initial interview in 1992. The AHEAD sub-sample consists of people born in 1923 or earlier, were household residents in the spring of 1992 and were still household residents in 1993 or 1994, and their spouses or partners at the time of the initial interview. The War Baby (WB) sub-sample of 2002 consists of people born during the period 1942-1947, were household residents in the spring of 1992, and who, at that time, did not have a spouse or partner born either before 1924 or between 1931 and 1941. They also were interviewed if they were still household residents at the time of the initial interview in 1998. The Children of the Depression (CODA) sub-sample consists of people born between the years 1924 and 1930 inclusive, were household residents at the time, in 1998, at the first interview, and who, at that time, did not have a spouse or partner who was born either before 1924 or between 1931 and 1947.

Baseline interviews and interviews for newly added sub-samples are conducted in-home, face-to-face. Telephone interviews are conducted every second year, with proxy interviews after death. Exceptions are made when respondents have health limitations, making an hour-plus session on the telephone difficult, or when there was no telephone in the household. Proxy informants were interviewed when the individual was unable to complete an interview due to physical or cognitive limitations. When a proxy interview was needed, the interviewers attempted to interview the person who was most familiar with the financial, health, and family situation of the sampled individual. The relationship of the proxy is noted in a variable that is present for each wave. A special questionnaire, which is referred to the "exit" interview, was developed to obtain an interview with an appropriate informant following the death of each sample member.

The RAND HRS Data file is a cleaned, easy-to-use, and a streamlined version of the Health and Retirement Study. The variables cover a broad, but not complete, range of measures. The file includes imputations for income, assets, and medical expenditures that were developed at RAND. The Data file is based on 1992, 1993, 1994, 1995, 1996, 1998, and 2000 final release of data and the 2002 preliminary release of data. The data in this file consists of all cohorts included in the HRS. The file contains a number of wealth and income variables and, where missing, values are imputed, resulting in more complete information regarding income and asset variables.

These features of the Rand HRS Data file make it a valuable resource, and this project makes use of these features. First, the age range of the respondents allows analyses that include both younger women and older women (i.e., at least age 50). This allows an examination into the income sources available for women at different stages of their lives. Women who either have just entered retirement or have access to Social Security retirement benefits can be compared and contrasted to those women who may still be working. Second, this project makes use of the non-white sub-samples in the file, since race is an important indicator of income security for women. Third, information is available for women across the different marital statuses that are of interest in this project. Finally, the complete and robust income and asset information available for all respondents and their spouses make this particularly useful for a study of income security for women.

Appendix 2: Statistical Tables

Table 1: Description of Dependent Variables: Total Household Income and Total Net Worth.[1]

Variable	Description
TOTAL HOUSEHOLD INCOME	Sum of all income in household
Wage and salary income.	The sum of respondent's wage/salary income, bonuses/overtime pay/commissions/tips, second job or military reserve earnings, professional practice or trade income.
Pension and annuity	The sum of all respondent's income from all pensions and annuities.
Social Security Retirement.	Respondent's income from Social Security retirement, spouse, or widow benefits.
Social Security disability or SSI.	The sum of the respondent's income from Social Security disability (SSDI) and Supplemental Security income (SSI).
Other government transfers.	Sums the income from veterans' benefits, welfare, and food stamps.
Unemployment and worker's compensation.	Sums the respondent's income from unemployment and worker's compensation.
Household capital income	The sum of household business or farm income, self-employment earnings, business income, gross rent, dividend and interest income, and other asset income.

Table 1: Description of Dependent Variables: Total Household Income and Total Net Worth.[1]

Other household income	Sums alimony, other income, lump sums from insurance, pensions, and inheritance.
TOTAL NET WORTH (WEALTH) *Assets:*	The sum of all wealth components less all debt.
Value of real estate	The reported or imputed net value of real estate that is not primary residence.
Transportation	Net value of vehicles.
IRA, Keogh accounts.	Net value of IRA/ Keogh accounts.
Business	Net value of business that respondent may own.
Stocks	The reported or imputed net value of stocks and mutual funds
Bonds	The net value of bonds or bond funds
Checking, savings accounts.	The reported or imputed value of checking, savings, and money market accounts.
CDs, Savings Bonds, and T-Bills	Net value of CDs, government savings, bonds, and treasury bills
Other savings.	Net value of other savings or assets, such as jewelry, or a collection for investment purposes.

Table 1: Description of Dependent Variables: Total Household Income and Total Net Worth.[1]

Primary residence	The reported or imputed value of respondent's primary residence or present value of home.
Debt:	
Mortgage	The reported or imputed value of all mortgages, both first and second.
Other home loans	Sums the reported outstanding balances of all home equity loans and lines of credit.
Other debt	The value of other debt such as credit card balances, medical debts, life insurance loans, or loans from relatives.

1. The source of data is the Rand HRS 2002 Data file, version D.

Table 2: Means and standard deviations of characteristics of women by marital status.[1]

Variable[2]	Married Means[3]	(s.d.)	Divorced Means	(s.d)	Widowed Means	(s.d)	Never married Means	(s.d)
Demographics								
Age in years	65.7	(8.6)	65.7	(8.4)	76.3	(10.2)	69.3	(10.7)
Years of education	12.4	(2.9)	12.2	(3.2)	11.2	(3.3)	12.3	(3.7)
Number of children	3.6	(2.1)	3.3	(2.1)	3.3	(2.1)	1.9	(2.1)
Employment history								
Currently working	.34	(.5)	.42	(.5)	.14	(.3)	.33	(.5)
Longest job tenure	15.3	(10.6)	15.3	(10.9)	18.0	(11.7)	20.7	(13.0)
Job status	2.4	(2.0)	2.2	(1.5)	2.7	(2.4)	2.1	(1.4)
Years worked	25.9	(14.8)	30.0	(14.7)	24.0	(17.3)	32.5	(15.6)
N	5449		1282		3346		308	

1. The source of data is the Rand HRS 2002 Data file, version D.
2. See text for description of variables.
3. Numbers are rounded to the nearest dollar amount.

Table 3: Means and standard deviations of total household income (n= 10,389).[1]

Variable	Means	Standard Deviation
Wage and salary income	$7,585	18680
Pension and annuity	2,950	15681
Social Security Disability	410	1713
Social Security Retirement	5,300	5359
Unemployment and Workers Compensation	47	582
Other government transfers	215	1468
Household capital income	10,742	81345
Other Household Income	2117	25196
TOTAL HOUSEHOLD INCOME	$46,262	97900

1. See table 2 notes.

Table 4: Means and Standard Deviations of Total Net Worth (n= 10,389)[1]

Variable	Means	Standard Deviation
Assets:		
Other Real Estate	$37,611	493225
Business	28,724	255068
Stocks	46,765	194512
Bonds	8,046	69887
Checking, savings Accounts	23,240	67036
CDs, Savings bonds, T-bills	12,317	51124
Transportation	12,229	21463
Total IRA	39,052	129790
Other savings	8,512	61674
Primary residence	121,561	252817
Debt:		
Total mortgage	17,965	48890
Other loans	1,878	11490
Other debt	2,474	16114
Total Net Worth	315,741	798451

1. See table 2 notes.

Table 5: Means and standard deviation of sources of income by marital status of women[1]

Variable	Married Means (s.d.)	Divorced Means (s.d)	Widowed Means (s.d.)	Never Married Means (s.d.)
Wage and salary income	$9091 ($20752)	$12720 ($21515)	$2857 ($10899)	$10892 ($22983)
Pension and annuity	2192 (18143)	2804 (7439)	4021 (12379)	5349 (23422)
Social Security Disability	270 (1452)	888 (2398)	388 (1630)	1130 (2660)
Social Security Retirement	3664 (4584)	3978 (5121)	8512 (5172)	4820 (5493)
Unemployment and work. comp.	53 (606)	88 (865)	25 (400)	26 (226)
Other government transfers	36 (676)	211 (1144)	513 (2291)	165 (769)
Household capital income	15297 (49065)	4063 (21670)	4307 (17408)	27948 (41786)
Other household income	2645 (28437)	1639 (17342)	1534 (23075)	1108 (7772)
Spouse income	31,434 (39311)	n/a	n/a	n/a
TOTAL HOUSEHOLD INCOME	64682 (79912)	26391 (35106)	22157 (35277)	51438 (421755)
TOTAL N	5449	1286	3346	308

1. See table 2 notes.

Table 6: Means and standard deviations of total net worth by marital status of women age 50 and older[1]

	Married		Divorced		Widowed		Never married	
	Means	(s.d.)	Means	(s.d.)	Means	(s.d.)	Means	(s.d)
Assets:								
Other real estate	$51,173	($399,481)	$47,112	($112,175)	$14,814	(105,560)	$5,664	($30,898)
Business	43,269	(299,291)	17,275	(344,199)	11,740	(99,169)	3,722	(27,094)
Stocks	65,420	(237,855)	17,659	(72,985)	29,540	(146,534)	25,380	(81,115)
Bonds	11,965	(88,694)	1,912	(18,742)	4,443	(44,836)	3,466	(41,251)
CDs, savings bonds, t-bills	15,164	(61,294)	4,140	(20,609)	10,859	(39,574)	11,945	(49,812)
Checking, savings accounts	29,963	(79,241)	11,697	(39,304)	17,660	(53,201)	13,135	(39,050)
Transportation	18,574	(26,266)	6,637	(14,410)	4,766	(9,139)	4,403	(7,247)
Total IRA	62,655	(165,552)	17,069	(77,418)	10,515	(54,648)	23,282	(71,518)
Primary residence	161,227	(318,482)	80,350	(127,244)	77,696	(144,427)	68,433	(94,264)
Other savings	11,743	(76,817)	6,212	(50,662)	4,378	(33,089)	5,849	(30,302)
Debt:								
Total mortgage	25,294	(58,342)	17,188	(44,968)	6,660	(27,767)	14,378	(35,352)
Other loans	2,841	(14,612)	1,009	(6,188)	722	(6,325)	1,047	(6,839)
Other debt	3,233	(18,921)	2,537	(10,272)	1,231	(13,190)	2,290	(8,337)
TOTAL NET WORTH	439,785	(861,312)	189,327	(124,311)	177,797	(346,344)	147,567	(236,685)
N	5449		1286		3346		308	

1. See Table 1a notes.

Table 7: Percentage of means of total household income by marital status

	Married	Divorced	Widowed	Never married
Wage and salary	14.1%	47.0%	12.9%	21.2%
Pension	3.4	11.0	18.1	10.4
Social Security disability	.4	3.4	1.8	2.2
Social Security retirement	5.7	15.1	38.4	9.4
Unemployment/worker's compensation	.1	.4	.1	.1
Other government transfers	.1	.8	2.3	.3
Household capital income	23.6	16.0	19.4	54.3
Other income	4.0	6.3	7.0	2.1
Spouse's income	48.6	n/a	n/a	n/a
Total	**100%**	**100%**	**100%**	**100%**

Table 8: Percentage of means of household assets by marital status

	Married	Divorced	Widowed	Never Married
Real estate	10.9%	22.4%	7.9%	3.4%
Business	9.2	8.2	6.4	2.3
Stocks	14.0	8.4	15.8	15.4
Bonds	2.5	1.0	2.4	2.0
CDs, savings bonds, and t-bills	3.2	1.9	5.8	7.2
Checking and savings	6.3	5.7	9.5	8.0
Vehicles	4.0	3.0	2.6	3.0
IRA	13.2	8.1	5.6	14.1
Primary residence	34.2	38.3	41.7	41.1
Other savings	2.5	3.0	2.3	3.5
Total	100%	100%	100%	100%

Table 9: Correlation Coefficients of Total Income and Total Wealth by Characteristics of Women

	Married		Divorced		Widowed		Never Married	
	Income	Wealth	Income	Wealth	Income	Wealth	Income	Wealth
Education	.239***	.228***	.326***	.083**	.240***	.260***	.104*	.323***
Age								
50-64	-.119***	-.008	.115***	.018	.113***	-.024	.091	.007
65-74	-.062***	.010	-.071*	-.022	.046**	.015	-.048	.012
75-84	-.072***	.002	-.043	.013	-.046**	.015	-.034	-.017
85+	-.029*	-.010	-.058*	-.015	-.088***	-.012	-.030	-.007
White	.069***	.120***	.090**	.059	.097***	.175***	.060	.334***
Race (1=African American)	-.065***	-.108***	-.083***	-.059*	-.093***	-.167***	-.053	-.303***
Race (1 = Hispanic)	-.087***	-.098***	-.120***	-.040*	-.079***	-.077***	-.029	-.107*
Number of children	-.062***	-.079***	-.101***	.019	-.032*	-.079***	-.134*	-.111
Working for pay	.190***	-.022	.287***	-.017	.217***	.039*	.110*	.099*
Job History	-.031*	.043**	-.065*	-.013	-.007	.019	-.008	-.030
Longest job tenure	.083***	.069***	.163***	.069*	.074***	.116***	-.061	.129*
Years worked	.098***	.069***	.171***	.010	.104***	.046**	.070	.295***
N	5449		1286		3346		308	

***p < .01 **p < .05 *p < .10

Table 10: Correlation Coefficients of Income Variables by Characteristics of Married Women (N=5449)

	Wages	Pension	Social Security Disability	Social Security Retirement	Unemployed. /workers comp.	Government transfers	HH capital income	Other household income	Spouse's Income
Education	.026***	.077***	-.082***	.028*	.017	-.015	.168***	.045**	.216***
Age									
50-64	-.331***	-.053***	.071***	-.607***	.078***	-.005	.075***	.032*	.175***
65-74	-.198***	.020	-.036**	.409***	-.051***	.002	-.038**	-.010	-.096***
75-84	-.176***	.048***	-.049***	.275***	-.036**	.003	-.049***	-.027*	-.097***
85+	-.061***	-.003	-.005	.086***	-.012	.007	-.013	-.012	-.051***
White	-.007	.009	-.080***	.075***	-.013	.005	.075***	.023	.072***
African American	.012	-.002	.081***	-.060***	.008	-.003	.078***	-.019	-.064***
Hispanic	-.054***	-.022	.010	-.058***	-.009	.017	-.067***	-.025*	-.087***
Children	-.059***	-.012	.041**	.022	.001	.000	-.041**	-.027*	-.087***
Working	.530***	-.045**	-.117***	-.294***	.032*	-.009	.076***	.005	.092***
Job history	-.093***	-.006	-.027	.095***	-.020	-.003	.003	-.020	.013
Job tenure	.115***	.078***	-.041**	.126***	.001	.007	.023	.001	-.056***
Years worked	.217***	.062***	-.029*	.056***	.039**	.006	.006	.011	-.001

***$p < .01$
**$p < .05$
*$p < .10$

Table 11: Correlation Coefficients of Income Variables by Characteristics of Divorced Women (N = 1286).

	Earnings	Pension	Social Security Disability	Social Security Retirement	Unemployment and workers comp.	Government transfers	Household capital income	Other household income
Education	.302***	.276***	-.230***	.016	-.202	-.082**	.130***	.041
Age								
50-64	-		.071*	-.618***	.051*	-.007	.007	-.008
65-74	.360***	.104***	-.050	.404***	-.024	.007	-.018	-.013
	-.210***	.094**						
75-84	-.194***	.028	-.005	.277***	-.035	-.006	.018	.041
85+	-.109***	-.006	-.059*	.169***	-.019	.011	-.006	-.041
White	.059*	-.041	-.082**	.095**	.001	-.003	.080**	.011
African American	-.035	.053*	.059*	-.064*	-.010	.005	-.078**	.169
Hispanic	-.083**	-.097**	.069*	-.052*	-.001	.045	-.053*	-.031
Children	-.122***	.117***	.086**	.006	.607	.042	-.001	-.028
Working	.528***	-.105***	-.276***	-.283***	.009	-.073**	.087**	-.013
Job history	-.080**	-.030	.128***	-.014	-.029	-.004	-.028	.003
Job tenure	.083**	.239***	-.156***	.151***	-.039	-.072*	.081**	.001
Years worked	.180***	.139***	-.295***	.152***	.000	-.066*	.050*	.003

***$p < .01$ **$p < .05$ *$p < .10$

Table 12: Correlation Coefficients of Income Variables by Characteristics of Widowed Women (N=3346)

	Wages	Pension	Social Security Disability	Social Security Retirement	Unemployment and workers comp.	Government transfers	HH capital income	Other household income
Education	.138***	.187***	-.168***	.156***	.018	.027	.147***	.065***
Age								
50-64	.351***	-.050**	.148***	-.442***	.045*	.021	.068***	.069***
65-74	.045**	.049**	.039*	.035*	.014	.000	.020	-.003
75-84	-.162***	.050**	-.088***	.182***	-.014	.028	.047**	-.021
85+	-.147***	-.065***	-.061***	.118***	-.036*	-.048**	-.023	-.029*
White	-.036*	.052**	-.106***	.235***	.009	-.008	-.088***	.028
African American	.024	-.062**	.105***	-.206***	-.005	.020	-.085***	-.085
Hispanic	-.013	-.062**	.083***	-.133***	-.005	-.023	-.049**	-.018
Children	.026	-.076**	.085***	-.115***	.025	.015	-.003	.001
Working (1 = yes)	.568***	-.028	-.082***	-.207***	.092***	-.013	.124***	.036*
Job history	-.061**	.009	.001	.079***	.006	.006	.008	-.011
Job tenure	.710	.146***	-.085***	.131***	-.021	-.023	.063	-.015
Years worked	.186***	.058***	-.070***	.013	.017	-.019	.045*	.010

***p < .01   **p < .05   *p < .10

Table 13: Correlation Coefficients of Income Variables by Characteristics of Never Married Women (N=308)

	Wages	Pension	Social Security Disability	Social Security Retirement	Unemployment and workers compensation	Government transfers	Household capital income	Other household income
Education	.266***	.185**	-.256***	.109*	.008	-.054	.079	.112*
Age								
50-64	.454***	.014	.087	-.627***	.139*	.133*	.071	.132*
65-74	-.204***	-.024	.056	.267***	-.076	-.041	-.039	-.052
75-84	-.193***	.019	-.120*	.292***	-.052	-.059	-.027	-.064
85+	-.174**	-.009	-.073	.233***	-.042	-.074	-.022	-.053
White	-.066	.117*	-.308***	.215***	-.108*	-.234***	.048	.097
African American	-.042	-.109*	-.320***	-.257***	.125*	.264***	-.043	-.085
Hispanic	-.047	-.066	.100*	-.123	-.036	.022	-.021	-.033
Children	-.081	-.111	.165*	-.194	-.006	.130	-.060	.017
Working	.545***	.029	-.235***	-.381***	.066	-.079	.086	.002
Job history	-.039	-.014	.010	.026	-.040	-.013	-.005	-.017
Job tenure	-.094	.086	-.147*	.233***	-.097	-.114*	-.063	-.024
Years worked	.191***	.096*	-.361***	.150**	.014	-.223***	.055	.057

***p < .01 **p < .05 *p < .10

Table 14: Correlation Coefficients of Wealth Variables by Characteristics of Married Women (N=5449)

	Real estate	Business	Stocks	Bonds	Checking	CDs	Vehicle	Other Savings	IRA	Home	Debt	Mortgage	Other Loans
Education	.061***	.039**	.180***	.107***	.151***	.060***	.187***	.101***	.204***	.179***	.023*	.176***	.064***
Age													
50-64	.012	.034*	-.026*	-.038**	-.039**	-.104**	.088***	.014	.004	.028*	.063***	.234***	.058***
65-74	-.003	-.015	.002	.018	.015	.041**	-.013	.005	.047**	-.022	-.126**	-.126**	-.005
75-84	-.012	-.024	.030	.023*	.035*	.080***	-.089**	-.018	-.053**	-.002	-.138**	-.138**	-.064**
85+	-.001	-.007	.009	.018	.000	.029*	-.041**	-.018	-.037**	-.024	-.059**	-.059**	-.027
White	.028*	.035**	.087***	.043**	.089***	.078***	.084***	.048***	.113***	.064***	-.021	-.005	.035*
African American	-.024	-.029*	-.080***	-.039**	-.080***	-.067**	-.084***	-.043**	-.101***	-.063***	.005	-.004	-.029
Hispanic	-.026*	-.036**	-.065***	-.037**	-.072***	-.063**	-.107**	-.031*	-.087***	-.054**	-.009	-.021	-.030*
Children	-.030	-.019	-.053**	-.029*	-.059***	-.062**	-.045**	.005	-.075**	-.039**	.020	-.021	-.035
Working	-.019	.060***	-.043**	-.055**	-.047***	-.077**	.045**	.005	-.033	.035	.027	.191***	.080**
Job History	.009	-.010	.035**	.034*	.051***	.037**	-.020	.017	.015	.034*	-.033*	-.051**	-.024
Job Tenure	.015	.047**	.036*	.012	.033*	.045**	.029*	.004	.054***	.051**	-.032*	-.047**	.010
Years worked	-.006	.018	-.031*	-.036**	-.017	-.029*	.064**	-.007	.043**	-.001	.003	.071***	.039**

***p < .01
**p < .05
*p < .10

Table 15: Correlation Coefficients of Wealth Variables by Characteristics of Divorced Women (N=1286).

	Real estate	Business	Stocks	Bonds	Checking	CDs	Vehicles	Other Savings	IRA	Home	Debt	Mortgage	Other Loans
Education	.024	.011	.186***	.046	.176***	.101***	.193***	.114***	.132***	.324***	.082**	.206***	.076**
Age													
50-64	.030	-.026	.018	.011	-.017	-.044	.108***	-.039	-.004	.052	.078**	.139***	.033
65-74	-.022	-.015	-.007	-.020	.003	-.040	-.042	.020	.037	-.019	-.028	-.070*	.014
75-84	-.011	.070	-.014	.021	.013	.086**	-.064*	.040	-.028	-.013	-.062*	-.085**	-.055*
85+	-.005	-.009	-.007	-.016	.018	.077**	-.078**	-.014	-.041	-.072	-.036	-.056*	-.030
White	.019	.024	.108***	.064*	.108***	.086**	.084**	.054*	.116***	.135***	.013	.004	.009
African American	-.021	-.025	-.110**	-.05*	-.098***	-.066*	-.082**	-.050*	-.098**	-.130***	-.002	-.017	-.002
Hispanic	-.014	-.011	-.085**	-.035	-.090**	-.063*	-.091**	-.041	-.070*	-.094**	-.046	-.031	-.013
Children	.034	.014	-.033	-.038	-.011	-.051*	-.011	-.037	-.032	-.100***	-.046	-.035	-.002
Working	-.022	-.016	-.033	.014	-.009	.013	.106***	-.006	.046*	.131***	.100***	.183***	.084**
Job History	-.005	-.023	.005	.001	.029	-.003	-.035	-.011	-.014	-.033	-.017	-.029	-.013
Job Tenure	.045	.012	.069*	-.002	.062*	.065*	.048	.056*	.026	.166***	-.033	.092**	.026
Years worked	.008	-.061*	.020	-.029	.056*	.071*	.064*	.018	.062*	.141***	.032	.088**	.061*

***p < .01
**p < .05
*p < .10

Table 16: Correlation Coefficients of Wealth Variables by Characteristics of Widowed Women (N=3346)

	Real estate	Business	Stocks	Bonds	Checking	CDs	Vehicle	Other Savings	IRA	Home	Debt	Mortgage	Other Loans
Education	.064***	.057**	.154***	.077***	.150***	.130***	.235***	.106***	.133***	.201***	.052**	.099***	.030*
Age													
50-64	-.015	.012	-.032*	.010	-.045**	-.072**	.111***	-.010	.056**	.013	.065***	.116***	.016
65-74	.032*	-.007	-.033*	-.013	-.017	-.045**	.134***	.034*	.059**	.056**	.036*	.075***	.046**
75-84	-.026	.004	-.034*	-.034*	.009	.057**	-.029*	-.005	.023	-.040*	-.077**	-.024	
85+	.008	-.007	.044*	.044*	.043*	.041*	-.193**	-.017	-.100***	-.093***	-.045*	-.084**	-.033*
White	.051**	.043*	.089***	.048**	.128***	.113***	.110***	.061***	.082***	.106***	-.012	-.050**	.005
African American	-.050**	-.043*	-.082**	-.045**	-.116***	-.104**	-.108**	-.058**	-.077**	-.107**	.015	.042*	.000
Hispanic	.000	-.015	-.045*	-.027	-.074***	-.066**	-.075**	-.027	-.037*	-.049**	-.001	.007	-.019
Children	-.019	-.026	-.042*	-.024	-.065***	-.067**	-.045*	-.008	-.026	-.046*	.011	.025	-.011
Working (1=yes)	.051**	.046**	-.022	-.015	-.012	-.042*	.161***	.012	.043*	.074***	.104***	.125***	.044*
Job History	.018	-.009	.009	.000	.009	.030*	-.019	-.004	.005	.018	.019	-.008	.016
Job Tenure	.071**	.089***	.044*	.012	.068**	.061**	.041	.046	-.007	.064**	.018	-.013	.015
Years worked	.029*	.029*	.002	.004	.011	-.028	.119***	.044*	.041*	.060***	.047**	.093***	.037*

***p < .01   **p < .05   *p < .10

Table 17: Correlation Coefficients of Wealth Variables by Characteristics of Never Married Women (N=308)

	Real estate	Business	Stocks	Bonds	Checking	CDs	Vehicle	Other Savings	IRA	Home	Debt	Mortgage	Other Loans
Education	.092	.107*	.222***	-.038	.169**	.131*	.328***	.162**	.148***	.318***	.023	.171**	.050
Age													
50-64	-.047	.100*	-.022	-.062	-.002	-.060	.116	.083	.031	.154**	.117	.312***	.048
65-74	.006	-.020	-.027	-.036	-.028	-.003	.052	.004	.064	-.008	.020	-.115*	.032
75-84	.052	-.062	-.009	-.027	.065	.080	-.062	-.052	-.020	-.120*	-.090	-.140*	-.069
85+	.002	-.051	.082	.176***	-.032	.003	-.177	-.071	-.115	-.083	-.100	-.147*	-.038
White	.026	.065	.205***	.062	.162**	.110*	.289***	.139	.227***	.269***	-.076	.095*	-.052
African American	-.058	-.071	-.206***	-.055	-.163**	-.088	-.248***	-.123	-.200***	-.210***	.095*	-.068	.052
Hispanic	.043	-.044	-.089	-.026	-.048	-.074	-.102*	-.014	-.064	-.071	-.007	-.019	-.032
Children	-.063	.004	-.069	-.071	.000	-.080	.024	.036	-.112	.025	-.106	.106	.041
Working (1=yes)	-.016	.175**	.053	-.052	-.007	-.004	.211***	.099	.028	.251***	-.138*	.292***	.186**
Job History	-.015	.026	-.025	-.007	-.030	.010	-.046	-.016	-.027	-.025	-.028	-.012	-.012
Job Tenure	-.016	-.065	.061	.119*	.071	.118	-.016	.023	.133	.007	.046	-.093	-.036
Years worked	.081	.061	.162**	.073	.159**	.110*	.240***	.103*	.205***	.250***	-.137*	.108*	.043

***p < .01 **p < .05 *p < .10

Table 18: OLS Regression Predicting Total Household Income of Marital Status Groups: Effects of Characteristics of the Women

Variable	Married B	β	Divorced B	β	Widowed B	β	Never Married B	β
Age	-4858.0***	-.058	-1137.8	-.026	-2878.2***	-.080	-14287.8	-.035
Years of Education	4556.0***	.203	2802.2***	-.072	1983.3***	.187	7326.9	.065
African American	-14301.5***	-.065	-5978.8**	-.072	-7876.5***	-.086	-37042.2	-.040
Hispanic	-938.4	-.004	-220.3	-.002	-3855.1	-.028	-15653.5	-.011
Number of children	-113.4	-.004	-11.0	-.001	57.2	.003	10342.1	.042
Employment history								
Currently working	18801***	.135	14782.3***	.208	16773.6***	.165	55777.0	.062
Job history	-441.56	-.013	-1086.5*	-.048	75.9	.005	1172.7	.004
Job Tenure	426.82***	.063	460.3***	.137	272.5***	.076	-2255.7	-.065
Years worked	-93.45	-.021	-14.8	-.006	-41.3	-.020	1230.2	.045
Intercept	-22837.6***		-15037.7*		2669.3		-39208.5	
N	5449		1286		3346		308	
R^2	.089		.173		.105		.027	

***p < .01 **p < .05 *p < .10

Table 19: OLS Regression Predicting Total Net Worth of Marital Status Groups: Effects of Characteristics of the Women

	Married		Divorced		Widowed		Never Married	
	B	β	B	β	B	β	B	β
Age	-30033.4*	-.028	-62455.4	-.040	-2403.5	-.007	-14205.5	-.062
Years of Education	65504.3***	.224	32679.9*	.084	24326.8***	.233	13724.3***	.216
African American	-262482.5***	-.091	-217258.6*	-.074	-122284.7***	-.136	-128296.5***	-.249
Hispanic	-67077.0	-.021	-112614.6	-.028	-14681.4	-.011	-30135.1	-.037
Number of children	-8012.2	-.019	30473.8*	.051	-1381.7	-.008	16346.8*	.120
Employment history								
Currently working	-90441.0**	-.050	-131366.4	-.052	17332.9	.017	-1493.2	-.003
Job history	5510.3	.013	-21529.4	-.027	562.7	.004	-2233.4	-.014
Job Tenure	6145.7***	.070	10432.0**	.088	3387.9***	.096	1777.0	-.092
Years worked	-3757.8**	-.065	-1868.2	-.022	-636.4	-.032	2118.2*	.139
Intercept	-245075.5**		-149665.6		-111283.1**		-93883.6	
N	5449		1286		3346		308	
R²	.071		.021		.093		.213	

***p < .01 **p < .05 *p < .10

Index

Note: Page numbers followed by "t" indicate material in tables.

AARP (American Association of Retired Persons), xi–xii, 138
African American women
    as category in study, 77–78
    demographic and social factors in women's wealth, 62–69, 114, 116, 121–122
    divorce and, 10, 98–99, 107
    hypotheses concerning, 79, 121–122
    income and marital status of, 97
    life patterns of, 18–19
    poverty and, 18–19, 32
    as single, never-married women, 102, 111–112
    as single mothers, 57, 59
    Social Security disability benefits and, 102–103
    total household income and, 94, 97, 98–99, 121–122
    wealth and, 105
    as widows, 100, 109
age
    categories for study, 77
    of divorced women, 7, 106–107, 176t
    at first marriage, 4, 5
    income inequality and, 133
    as independent variable in study, 77, 113, 116, 118–119, 127
    life expectancy, 16–17
    of married women, 104–105, 176t
    as mediating factor, 2, 16–18
    poverty and, 7, 11, 12–14, 17–18, 21, 32
    of retirement, 19
    of single, never-married women, 102, 111, 176t
    total household income and, 94, 102
    wealth and, 104–105
    of widowed women, 7, 11–14, 21, 108–109, 176t
    See also older women
Allianz Insurance survey, 139
Altobelli, J., 31, 124
Amato, P. R., 50, 51–52
American Association of Retired Persons (AARP), xi–xii, 138
Amsterdam. *See* Netherlands
Arditti, J. A., 53
Australia
    economic dependency of women, 48
    health and social needs of older women in, 35

baby-generation, xii, 50, 61, 138, 139
Bangladesh, economic differences by gender in well-being, 66–67
Bank of Italy Survey, 49
Baumann, K. J., 5, 58
Behringer, A., 38–39

Belgium, employment history of mothers, 47
Bianchi, S. M., 9, 48, 125, 127–128
Biddlecom, A. E., 37
Binney, E., 25
black women. *See* African American women; South Africa
Bound, J., 12
Brandon, P. D., 44–45
Brazil, employment history of women and, 49–50
Brooks-Gunn, J., 5, 59
Bureau of Labor Statistics Consumer Expenditure Survey, 61–62
Burkhauser, R., 7, 9, 11–12, 17
Butrica, B. A., 50
Byles, J. E., 35

Cain, B. S., 10, 15
Campbell, R. T., 132
Canada
    comparisons of married and unmarried women in, 34
    economic dependency of women, 48
    economic well-being of married and divorced women in, 35–36
    gender differences in economic well-being, 67–68
    social role and health status of women in, 34–35
Cancian, M., 41
Casper, L. M., 48, 125, 127–128
Chang, K., 43–44
Cherlin, A. J., 9, 18
Chevan, A., 56

children
    adult, financial assistance for parents, 5, 6–7, 55, 67
    childcare decisions of married women, 44–45
    divorced women and, 9, 99, 107–108, 176t
    employment history of mother and, 20, 23, 39, 47, 68–69, 99, 107–108
    hypotheses concerning, 79, 122
    impact of divorce on, 9
    impact on mother's economic well-being, 68–69
    as independent variable in study, 78, 122
    of married women, 44–45, 97, 105, 176t
    as mediating factor, 2, 23
    number of, and employment history of mother, 20, 23, 39, 48
    poverty risks and, 20, 23, 64–65
    of single, never-married women, 103, 176t. *See also* single mothers
    total household income and, 94, 97, 101
    wealth and, 105
    of widowed women, 101, 110, 176t
    See also single mothers
Choi, N., 7, 21, 22
Choudhury, S., 3, 17
Clydesdale, T. T., 41–42
Consumer Expenditure Surveys, 33, 56, 60–62
credit card use, 138

cross-cultural comparisons
    demographic and social factors in women's wealth, 66–69, 71–72
    of married and unmarried women, 33–36
    of married women, 47–50
Crowder, K. D., 37–38
Crystal, S., 132
Current Population Survey, 39, 41, 53–54
Curtis, L., 34

Davies, H., 68–69
Davies, S., 35–36
de Barros, P., 49–50
DeBoer, D. D., 42
debt, levels of household, 89–90, 104–106, 107, 138
De Graaf, N. D., 48–49
Del Boca, D., 49
de Mendonca, P., 49–50
Denton, M., 35–36
DeViney, S., 3, 32–33, 46, 124
Dinkins, J. M., 61–62
divorced women
    adjustment to divorce, 51–52, 129–130
    age of, 7, 106–107, 176t
    as category in study, 77, 129–130
    causes of divorce, 52–53
    characteristics and income of, 50, 98–99
    characteristics and wealth of, 106–108
    children and, 9, 99, 107–108, 176t
    comparisons with married women, 30–36, 176t
    consumption and savings before divorce, 8, 56
    demographic and employment characteristics in study data, 81
    economic impact of divorce and, 31–32, 53–54
    economic well-being of, 8, 9–11, 17–18, 30–36, 50–54, 106–108
    education of, 106, 130, 176t
    employment history and, 20–21, 53–54, 98, 176t
    hypotheses concerning, 79, 119–120
    impact of marital status on wealth, 8, 9–11, 17–18
    literature review on, 30–36, 50–54
    poverty risks of, 7, 22, 53–54
    precursors of divorce, 41–43
    predicting income and wealth from background characteristics, 113–117, 192t, 193t
    psychosocial effects of divorce and, 15
    race/ethnicity of, 10, 98–99, 107
    remarriage and, 15–16, 31
    total household assets by marital status, 87–89, 91–93, 189t
    total household income of, 30–36, 50–54, 85, 90–91, 93–95, 185t
Dixon, C. S., 54
Dolan, M. A., 52–53
Duncan, G., 10, 12, 15, 17, 20

economic dependency, of married women, 47–49, 123–125, 127–128
economic well-being
    comparisons of married and unmarried women, 30–36
    defined, 1, 7–8
    as dependent variable for Rand Health and Retirement Study (HRS) data, 74–76
    of divorced women, 8, 9–11, 17–18, 30–36, 50–54, 106–108
    impact of children on mother's, 68–69
    impact of marriage on female, 1, 3–16, 17–18
    of married women, 5–6, 30–50, 103–106
    of single, never-married women, 4–5, 30–36, 57–62, 110–113
of widowed women, 8–10, 11–14, 17–18, 30–36, 54–56, 108–110
See also income of women; net worth; total household income; total household net worth (wealth); wealth of women
Edin, K., 59–60
education
    of divorced women, 106, 130, 176t
    human capital effect and, 116, 130
    hypotheses concerning, 120–121
    as independent variable in study, 78, 113, 115–116, 120–121, 130
    of married women, 96, 103–104, 113, 130, 176t
    as mediating factor, 2, 21–23
    poverty risks and, 22–23
    retirement income of divorced women, 50
    of single, never-married women, 4, 111, 131, 176t
    of single mothers, 57–62
    total household income and, 93–94, 96, 99–100, 113–117
    wealth and, 103–104
    of widowed women, 99–100, 108, 130, 176t
Edwards, M. E., 39
Elder, G. H., Jr., 24, 25, 132, 133
elderly women. *See* older women
employment history
    children and, 20, 23, 39, 47, 68–69, 99, 107–108
    cross-cultural studies of impact of, 47–50
    demographic and social factors in women's wealth, 63–69
    divorce and, 20–21, 53–54, 98, 176t
    economic dependency of women and, 47–49
    education and, 21–23
    ethnicity and, 18–19
    as independent variable in study, 78, 114, 116–117
    of married women, 20, 39–43, 96–97, 105–106, 125, 176t
    as mediating factor, 2, 20–21

of older women, 19, 20
of single, never-married women, 103, 112–113, 126, 176t
of single mothers, 57–62
total household income and, 95, 96–98, 100
wealth and, 105–106
of widowed women, 14, 20–21, 100, 110, 128–129, 176t
Enron, collapse of, xi, 137
Esping-Anderson, G., 48
Estes, C., 25, 26, 27, 134
ethnicity. See African American women; Hispanic women; race/ethnicity

Fan, J. X., 43–44
Feaster, D. J., 11
Feldman, S., 35
Feminist perspective, 26–27, 62–69, 123, 127, 134–135. See also Gender inequality
Fethke, C. C., 8
Finland, economic dependency of women, 48
Fitzpatrick, T. R., 45–46
Flavin, M. A., 8

Garfinkle, I., 9
gendered nature of society. See Feminist perspective
gender inequality
cross-cultural studies of, 66–69
demographic and social factors in women's wealth, 62–69
enduring nature of, 38–39
in retirement benefits, 32–33, 45–46, 67

See also Feminist perspective
General Social Surveys, 32
George, L. K., 24, 132
Georgia Centenarian Study, 32
Germany
economic dependency of women, 48
widowed women in, 54–55
Glick, P., 15
Goetting, M. A., 32, 126
Goodfellow, G., 9
Gough, O., 67
Great Britain
employment history of mothers, 47, 68–69
gender differences in economic well-being, 67, 68–69
Guadagno, M., 33
Gyamfi, P., 5, 59

Hanson, T. L., 50, 52, 120, 129
Hao, L., 8
Hardy, M. A., 5, 20, 63, 124
Harrington-Meyer, M., 14, 17, 21
Hatch, L., 23
head of household status, 37, 58, 69. See also single mothers
Health and Retirement Study. See Rand Health and Retirement Study (HRS)
Heckert, D. A., 43
Henretta, J. C., 6, 9, 20, 132, 133
Hirschl, T. A., 31, 124
Hispanic women
as category in study, 77–78
divorce and, 98–99, 107

hypotheses concerning, 79, 121–122
income and marital status of, 97
as single, never-married women, 112
Social Security disability benefits and, 102–103
total household income and, 98–99, 121–122
wealth and, 105
as widows, 100, 109–110
Hoffman, C. D., 52–53
Hoffman, S. D., 10, 15, 20
Hogan, R., 38–39, 66
Holden, K., 7, 9, 11, 12, 20
Holland. *See* Netherlands
home ownership
debt component of total household net worth and, 89–90, 104–106, 107
divorce and, 129–130
employment of young mothers and, 39
residential mobility of widows, 56
single, never-married women and, 133–134
single mothers and, 58, 60–61
total household net worth and, 84, 87, 133–134
HRS. *See* Rand Health and Retirement Study (HRS)
human capital effect, 116, 130
Hungerford, T. L., 11, 54–55
Hurd, M. D., 5, 11, 12

Iams, H. M., 50
income of women

comparisons of married and unmarried women, 30–36
divorced women, 30–36, 50–54
education and, 22–23
individual earnings, defined, 76
individual income from employer pension and annuity, defined, 76
individual income from other government transfers, defined, 76
individual income from Social Security Disability or SSI, defined, 76
individual income from Social Security retirement, defined, 76
marital happiness and, 42–43
by marital status, 30–36, 96–103, 179t, 184–187t
married women, 5, 30–50
power in marriage and, 37, 42
predicting from background characteristics, 113–117, 192t
single never-married, 4–5, 30–36, 57–62
single mothers, 57–62
trends in, xii–xiii
from unemployment and worker's compensation, defined, 76
widowed women, 30–36, 54–56
See also total household income

Indonesia, gender differences in economic well-being, 66–67
Integrated Public Use Microdata Series, 55
Italy, education and employment status of wives and husbands, 49

Jackson, A. P., 5, 59
Janzen, B. L., 34–35
job tenure
    of divorced women, 99, 116
    of married women, 98, 116–117
    of single, never-married women, 103, 112
    total household income and, 95, 98, 99, 114, 116
    of widows, 101
        See also employment history
Jones, S., 69, 71–72
Joshi, H., 68–69

Kart, C. S., 5
Kivett, V., 56
Knodel, J., 66–67
Knotter, A., 47
Koso, G., 8, 31, 126
Kramarow, E. A., 37
Kuo, D., 7

Labour Force Survey (Great Britain), 67
Landerman, R., 23
Laren, D. S., 12
Leonesio, M., 3, 17
Life Course perspective, 2–3, 24–25, 63–64, 123, 127, 132–134

life expectancy, 16–17
life insurance benefits, 13, 21
Lillard, L. A., 9
Lin, S., 15
Linkins, K., 25
Lino, M., 60–61
literature review, 29–72
    comparisons of married and unmarried women, 30–36
    cross-cultural studies, 33–35, 47–50, 66–69, 71–72
    divorced women, 30–36, 50–54
    married women, 30–50
    never married women, 30–36, 57–62
    widowed women, 30–36, 54–56
    women's income equality relative to men, 62–69
Locatelli, M., 49
Loew, R. M., 53–54
Luxembourg, economic dependency of women, 48

Malaysia, gender differences in economic well-being, 66–67
Mare, R. D., 40
marital dissolution
    impact on black women, 18–19
    income and education level in, 22
    precursors of divorce, 41–43
    psychosocial effects of, 3–4, 6–15
    remarriage and, 15–16, 31
    See also divorced women; widowed women

marital status
 characteristics and income by, 96–103
 characteristics and wealth by, 103–110
 divorced women. *See* divorced women
 economic well-being of women and, 1, 3–16
 as independent variable for study, 77
 marital dissolution, 3–4, 6–15
 married women. *See* married women
 pension/retirement benefits and, 85–89, 92–93, 96–98, 102, 106, 119–120, 128
 single, never-married women. *See* single, never-married women
 total household asset distribution and, 91–93, 182t
 total household income and, 84–87, 90–91, 93–103, 179t, 181t, 183t, 184t, 185t, 186t, 187t
 total household net worth and, 87–90, 180t, 183t
 transitions in, 2, 3–4, 6–9, 45–46
 wealth of women and, 1, 3–16, 30–36, 103–113
 widowed women. *See* widowed women
married women
 advantages of marriage and, 36–38, 71, 123–126
 age of, 104–105, 176t
 as category in study, 77, 123–126
 characteristics and income of, 96–98
 characteristics and wealth of, 103–106
 children of, 44–45, 97, 105, 176t
 comparisons with unmarried women, 30–36, 176t
 cross-cultural comparisons of, 47–50
 demographic and employment characteristics in study data, 81
 disadvantages of marriage and, 38–39, 59–60, 64–65, 69, 71–72, 116, 121–122, 131–132
 economic dependency of, 47–49, 123–125, 127–128
 economic well-being of, 5–6, 30–50, 103–106
 education of, 96, 103–104, 113, 130, 176t
 employment history of, 20, 39–43, 96–97, 105–106, 125, 176t
 hypotheses concerning, 79, 118–119
 impact of marital status on wealth, 5–6, 17–18
 literature review on, 30–50
 marital stability and, 40–43
 net worth of, 87–90
 precursors of divorce, 41–43
 predicting income and wealth from background characteristics, 113–117, 192t, 193t

Social Security spousal and survivor benefits, 5, 8–9, 12–14, 119
total household assets of, 91–93, 125–127, 188t
total household income of, 85, 90–91, 93–95, 124–125, 184t
See also children; divorced women; widowed women
Maudlin, T. A., 22
Maume, D. J., Jr., 62–63
McGarry, K., 55
McLanahan, S. S., 9, 48–49, 50, 52, 120, 129
McLaughlin, D. K., 65–66
McNamara, J. M., 11, 63–64, 127
McNamara, T. K., 19
Medicaid, 54
medical benefits, decline in, 137–138
Medical Expenditure Panel Surveys (MEPS), 44
Medicare, 64
Mishra, G., 35
Moen, P., 26, 134
Morgan, L. L., 7, 8, 11, 13–14, 19–22, 120, 129
Muhajarine, N., 34–35
Myers, D., 7, 11, 12
Myers, M., 10

National Consumer Law Center, 138
National Institute on Aging, 73
National Longitudinal Study of the High School Class of 1972, 44–45
National Longitudinal Surveys of Women, 40

National Survey of Families and Households (NSFH), 46, 52, 58
Nelson, D., 57
Netherlands
economic dependency of women, 48–49
employment history of mothers, 47
net worth
components of, 83
defined, 1, 83
by marital status, 87–90
See also total household net worth (wealth); wealth of women
never-married women. *See* single, never-married women
New Beneficiary Data, 64–65
Nieswiadomy, M. L., 5, 61
Normative Aging Study, 45–46
Norway
comparisons of married and unmarried women in, 34
economic dependency of women, 48
Nowak, T. C., 43

O'Bryant, S. L., 11
Ofstedal, M. B., 66–67
O'Grady-LeShane, R., 17
Old-Age-Survivors-and Disability Insurance (OASDI), 64
older women
categories for study, 77
cross-cultural comparisons of, 66–69
demographic and social factors in women's wealth, 63–69, 71
employment history of, 19, 20

ethnicity and, 18–19
health and social needs of, 35
impact of divorce on, 10–11, 22
impact of widowhood on, 11–14, 54–55
old, defined, 77
oldest old, defined, 77
poverty and, 7, 11, 12–14, 17–18, 21, 32
Social Security as main source of income for, 18, 21, 55, 65, 66
support from adult children, 5, 6–7, 55
young old, defined, 77
Olenick, L., 12
O'Rand, A., 2–3, 6, 9, 17, 20, 23, 24, 132, 133
Orman, S., xiii, 136–137, 138–139
other household income, by marital status of women in study, 85
Oygard, L., 50, 51
Ozawa, M. N., 64–65

Pandey, S., 57
Panel Study of Income Dynamics (PSID), 12–13, 31, 40, 43, 54–56, 57, 62–64
parenthood. *See* children
Pasqua, S., 49
patriarchal family forms, 27
Patton, R., 57
Peltola, P. K., 48, 125, 127–128
pension/retirement benefits
 company default on, xi–xii, 137
 decline in, xii, 137–138
 female participation in, xiii

gender differences in, 32–33, 45–46, 67
marital status and, 85–89, 92–93, 96–98, 102, 106, 119–120, 128
married women's access to spousal benefits, 5, 12–14, 32, 55
mean amount of retirement income, 83
retirement as family transition, 45–46
single mothers and, 61
splitting of accrued pension rights, 9
total household income and, 90–91, 98, 100
widows and, 101
See also Social Security system
Peronaci, R., 68–69
Perrucci, C. C., 38–39, 66
Peterson, R. R., 10
Pezzin, L., 5
Philippines, gender differences in economic well-being, 66–67
Phipps, S., 34
Political Economy of Aging perspective, 25–26, 123, 127, 134
Pollock, G. E., 7, 11, 15, 22, 31–32
poverty
 children and, 20, 23, 64–65
 demographic and social factors in women's wealth, 62–69
 divorced women and, 7, 22, 53–54
 education and, 22–23
 ethnicity and, 18–19, 32

following divorce, 17–19
after marital dissolution, 7, 17–18
older women and, 7, 11, 12–14, 17–18, 21, 32
race/ethnicity and, 18–19, 32
single mothers and, 57–62
in widowhood, 7, 11, 12–14, 17–18, 21, 55
See also single mothers
Prus, S., 67–68
PSID (Panel Study of Income Dynamics), 12–13, 31, 40, 43, 54–56, 57
Public Use Samples of the U.S. Census, 65–66

race/ethnicity
 demographic and social factors in women's wealth, 62–69, 114, 116, 121–122
 divorce and, 98–99, 107
 as independent variable in study, 77–78, 114, 116, 121–122, 131–132
 of married women, 97, 105
 as mediating factor, 2, 18–19
 poverty and, 18–19, 32
 retirement income of divorced women, 50
 of single, never-married women, 102, 111–112
 total household income and, 94, 97, 98–99, 102
 wealth and, 105
 widowhood and, 19, 100–101, 109–110
 See also cross-cultural comparisons of Hispanic women, African American women, and white women
Rand Health and Retirement Study (HRS), 73–122
 Advance Data File, xi–xiv, 123–125
 age as independent variable, 77
 described, 166–172
 descriptive statistics concerning women, 80–93
 economic well-being as dependent variable, 74–76
 education as independent variable, 78
 employment history as independent variable, 78
 ethnicity as independent variable, 77–78
 hypotheses concerning women, 79, 117–122
 marital status as independent variable, 77
 number of children as independent variable, 78
 sample size for study, 73
 women's characteristics and household income or wealth, 93–113
 women's characteristics in predicting total income and wealth, 113–117
Rank, M. R., 31, 124
Reed, D., 41
Reidy, E., 66–67
remarriage, 15–16, 31
retirement benefits. *See* pension/retirement benefits; Social Security system
Retirement History Study, 12
Rettig, K. D., 54

review of literature. *See* literature review
Rix, S. E., 65, 127
Rogers, S. J., 42–43
Roos, P. A., 27
Rubin, R. M., 5, 61
Ruble, M., 57

Scheiber, S., 9
Schoeni, R. F., 55
Schuchardt, J., 33
Schwenk, F., 56
Shaw, K., 39–40
Shea, D., 132
Sherraden, M., 58
Singapore, gender differences in economic well-being, 66–67
single, never-married women
    age of, 102, 111, 176t
    as category in study, 77, 126–127
    characteristics and income of, 101–103
    characteristics and wealth of, 110–113
    children of, 103, 176t
    comparisons with married women, 30–36, 176t
    consumption and savings patterns of, 56, 57, 58, 60–62
    demographic and employment characteristics in study data, 82
    economic well-being of, 4–5, 30–36, 57–62, 110–113
    education of, 4, 111, 131, 176t
    employment history of, 103, 112–113, 126, 176t
    home ownership of, 133–134
    hypotheses concerning, 79, 119–120
    impact of marital status on wealth, 4–5, 57–62
    increase in number of, 137
    literature review on, 30–36, 57–62
    net worth of, 87–89
    predicting wealth and income from background characteris-tics, 113–117, 192t, 193t
    race/ethnicity of, 102, 111–112
    sample size in study, 114–115, 126
    total household assets by marital status, 91–93, 191t
    total household income of, 4–5, 30–36, 57–62, 85, 86–87, 90–91, 187t
    See also single mothers
single mothers
    economic well-being of, 5, 9, 57–62, 71, 112
    education of, 57–62
    employment history of, 57–62
    geographic location of, 60–61
    head of household status, 37, 69
    home ownership and, 58, 60–61
    See also single, never-married women
Smith, K. R., 7, 13, 21
Smock, P. J., 7, 9, 11, 20–22
Snyder, K. A., 43

Social Security system
   changes in, xii, 137, 138
   disability benefits, race/ethnicity and, 102–103
   dual entitlement and, 6
   impact of, 17
   as main source of income for older women, 18, 21, 55, 65, 66, 126–129, 135, 137
   mean amount of retirement income, 83–87
   Social Security Administration Master Beneficiary Record, 32–33
   Social Security Administration Modeling Income in the Near Term (MINT1), 50
   survivor benefits of married women, 5, 8–9, 12–14, 119
   widows and, 100, 101
Solomon, J. C., 32–33, 124
Sorensen, A., 48–49
South Africa, men as economic liability in, 69, 71–72
Spouse's income, defined, 76
Statistic Canada Survey of Labor and Income Dynamics, 35–36
Steinberg-Schone, B., 5
Stirling, K. J., 10
Street, D., 8, 14, 18, 20, 26, 127, 132
Stroup, A. L., 7, 11, 15, 22, 31–32
Supplemental Security Income (SSI), 17, 32
Survey of Income and Program Participation, 58–59

Sweden, economic dependency of women, 48
Szinovacz, M. E., 46

Taiwan, gender differences in economic well-being, 66–67
Teachman, J. D., 37–38
Tedrow, L. M., 37–38
Thailand, gender differences in economic well-being, 66–67
Thomson, E., 50, 52, 120, 129
total household income
   for all women in study, 83, 177t
   characteristics of women in study and, 93–103, 184t
   components of, 74–75, 82–83, 90–91
   defined, 74
   as dependent variable for Rand Health and Retirement Study (HRS) data, 74–75, 173–174t
   by marital status of women in study, 84–87, 90–91, 93–103, 179t, 181t, 183t, 184t, 185t, 187t
   percentages of components by marital status, 90–91
   predicting from background characteristics, 113–117, 192t
   sources of income available, 75–76
   See also income of women
total household net worth (wealth)
   for all women in study, 84, 178t
   assets by marital status, 91–93, 182t

characteristics of women in study and, 93–95
components of, 75, 83
debt component of, 89–90, 104–106, 107, 138
defined, 75
as dependent variable for Rand Health and Retirement Study (HRS) data, 75–76, 174–175t
by marital status, 87–90, 180t, 183t
net worth, defined, 1, 83
predicting from background characteristics, 113–117, 193t
sources of income available, 75–76
See also net worth; wealth of women
Tseng, H., 64–65
Tzeng, J. M., 40

Uhlenberg, P., 10, 15–16
U.S. Bureau of the Census, ix, 17, 37, 65–66
U.S. Department of Labor, ix, xii–xiii

Van Berkel, M., 48–49
Vartanian, T. P., 11, 63–64, 127
Vietnam, gender differences in economic well-being, 66–67
Vinick, B., 45–46

Waite, L. J., 5, 9, 36–37
Wang, H., 50, 51–52
wealth of women
  comparisons of married and unmarried women, 30–36
  defined, 1–2
  demographic and social factors in women's wealth, 62–69
  divorced women, 8, 9–11, 30–36, 50–54, 106–108
  impact of marriage on, 1–2, 3–16, 17–18
  by marital status, 1, 3–16, 30–36, 103–113
  married women, 5–6, 30–50, 103–106
  predicting from background characteristics, 113–117, 193t
  single women, never-married, 4–5, 30–36, 57–62, 110–113
  single mothers, 57–62
  widowed women, 8–10, 11–14, 30–36, 54–56, 108–110
  See also net worth/wealth; total household net worth
Weitzman, L., 31–32
welfare states typology, 48
white women
  as category in study, 77–78
  Social Security disability benefits and, 102–103
widowed women
  age of, 7, 11–14, 21, 108–109, 176t
  as category in study, 77, 128–129
  characteristics and income of, 99–101
  characteristics and wealth of, 108–110
  children of, 101, 110, 176t
  comparisons with married women, 30–36, 176t

consumption and savings patterns prior to divorce, 8–9, 43–44, 56
demographic and employment characteristics in study data, 81–82
economic well-being of, 8–10, 11–14, 17–18, 30–36, 54–56, 108–110
education of, 99–100, 108, 130, 176t
employment history of, 14, 20–21, 110, 128–129, 176t
hypotheses concerning, 79, 119–120
impact of marital status on wealth, 8–10, 11–14, 17–18, 30–36, 54–56
literature review on, 30–36, 54–56
net worth of, 87–89
poverty risks of, 7, 11, 12–14, 17–18, 21, 55
predicting income and wealth from background characteristics, 113–117, 192t, 193t
psychosocial effects of widowhood, 15
race/ethnicity of, 19, 100–101, 109–110
remarriage and, 15–16, 31
residential mobility of, 56
total household assets by marital status, 91–93, 190t
total household income of, 30–36, 54–56, 85–86, 90–91, 93–95, 186t
Williamson, J. B., 19, 65, 127
Willson, A. E., 2, 3, 5, 18, 19, 20, 63, 124, 131, 132
Wilmoth, J., 8, 14, 18, 20, 26, 31, 126, 127, 132
Wise, D. A., 5, 11, 12
Women & Money (Orman), 136–137, 138–139
work history. *See* employment history; job tenure

Youth-Parent Socialization Panel, 41–42

Zhan, M., 57, 58
Zick, C. D., 7, 13, 21, 43–44

HQ 1381 .J69 2007
Joyce, Joyce A.
Women, marriage, and wealth

AUG 1 6 2007